The Conquest Of Fear

Wilder Publications, Inc.
PO Box 10641
Blacksburg, VA 24063

ISBN 10: 1-61720-299-1
ISBN 13: 978-1-61720-299-5
First Edition

10 9 8 7 6 5 4 3 2 1

The Conquest Of Fear

by Basil King

With A New Introduction By Henry C. Link

Contents

Introduction

There are many books which give some help to many people. There are books which give a set of rules, or even one master rule, by which to meet the problems of life. This is not such a book. It suggests no simple recipe for the conquest of fear. Instead, it presents, what all too few of us to-day possess, a philosophy of life.

Moreover, in contrast to the dominant thinking of our age, which is materialistic, King's philosophy is spiritual and religious. Indeed, the ideas in this book are so profoundly different from the commonly accepted ideas of our times that they will come as a shock to many readers. One purpose of this introduction is to prepare the reader for such a shock.

I have said that the dominant thinking of our age is materialistic, and by that I mean also physical. Let me illustrate this broad statement with reference to the subject of fears alone. The conquest of fear has gone on year after year chiefly through physical means. Physical pain has always been one of the great sources of fear. Now ether and other anaesthetics have eliminated the chief pains of major operations. Older people can still remember their fear of the dentist, when killing a nerve or pulling a tooth caused excruciating pain. Now local anaesthetics even in minor troubles have made dentistry almost painless. We have not conquered these fears of pain—rather their cause has been removed.

Twilight sleep, the artificial sleep to alleviate the pains of childbirth, is the perfect expression of the scientific and materialistic elimination of fear. By a chemical blackout of the mind, a dimming of the conscious self, the person is enabled to escape the necessity of facing and conquering fear through his own resources.

I am not condemning the physical alleviation of pain or the progress of physical science. I am only describing a trend, and that is the growing emphasis on the elimination of fears by science rather than on their conquest by the individual.

Illness has always been a great source of fear, and still is. The dread of cancer is one of the terrifying fears of our time and fortunes are spent in cancer research and education. The Conquest of Fear was written as a result of the author's threatened total blindness. He faced a fact for which there seemed no physical remedy—hence his great need for a spiritual conquest of this great fear.

And yet, year by year, physical science has been eliminating or reducing the dangers of sickness. Vaccines for the prevention of the dread disease, small-pox, are now a matter of course. Vaccines and specifics against the deadly tetanus, against typhoid fever, diphtheria, syphilis, and other fearful diseases have become commonplace. The fear of pneumonia has been almost eliminated through the discoveries of the miraculous sulpha drugs. Science has done wonders toward the elimination of such fears. A man need hardly conquer the fear of any particular sickness—there is left for his conquest chiefly the fear of dying.

In addition to physical disease, our civilization has now developed mental ailments of all kinds. These include a large category of fears called phobias—claustrophobia, agoraphobia, photophobia, altaphobia, phonophobia, etc.

Three fields or professions, other than religion and philosophy, have sought to deal with these fears, the psychiatric, the psychoanalytic, and the psychological. The medical psychiatric profession has naturally emphasized physical remedies beginning with sedatives and bromides to induce artificial relaxation and ending up with lobectomy or the complete cutting off of the frontal lobes of the brain, the centers of man's highest thought processes. Between these two extremes are the shock treatments in which an injection of insulin or metrazol into the blood stream causes the person to fall into a sort of epileptic fit during which he loses consciousness. Through a series of such shock treatments some of the higher nerve centers or nerve pathways are destroyed. By this process a person's fears may also be eliminated and he may be permanently or temporarily cured. In short, the person does not conquer the fears in his mind; the psychiatrist or neurologist, by physically destroying a part of the person's brain, destroys also the fears.

How strongly this physical approach has taken hold of people was made plain to me through an article of mine on how to conquer fears. The emphasis in this article was on how people could overcome their fears and worries through their own efforts. To illustrate the opposite extreme, I mentioned the brain operations and shock treatments by which psychiatry now often deals with fears. Among the many people who wrote to me as a result of this article, the majority inquired where they could obtain such an operation! To such extremes have many people gone in their desire to eliminate fear by physical means rather than conquer it through their own spiritual powers.

The psychoanalyst deals with a person's phobias through what seems like an intellectual or rational process. According to psychoanalysis, phobias or fears are due to some buried or subconscious complex. By daily or frequent talks with a psychoanalyst for a period of six months or a year, a person's subconscious disturbance may be brought to light, and if so, the fear is supposed automatically to disappear. Even if true, this process is a highly materialistic one, at least in the sense that only people who can spend thousands of dollars can afford such treatments.

The psychologist, as well as some psychiatrists who have studied normal psychology, regard many fears as normal experiences which the individual can cope with largely through his own resources and with very little help in the way of visits or treatment. The trouble arises in the case of those people who have no personal resources to draw on. Their lives are so lacking in spiritual power, or so full of intellectual scepticism and distrust, that they cannot help themselves. They have no religious convictions or certainties by which to obtain leverage in their struggles. They have no firm philosophy of life on which they or those who would help them can lay hold. They are putty in the hands of the fears and forces that beset them from without.

The psychologist and the psychiatrist both find it difficult to do much to help such a person. And yet, this is the kind of person our civilization and education tends increasingly to produce. By the physical elimination of the causes of fear we have gradually undermined man's inner resources for the conquest of fear.

This materialistic trend has received a new impetus from the fields of political science, economics, and sociology. A dozen years ago economic disaster threatened to stampede the nation. Millions who had lost their jobs began to fear penury and want. Millions who still had jobs feared that they would lose them. Other millions began to fear the loss of their money and possessions. Rich and poor, becoming afraid that the country was going to pieces, rushed to the banks to withdraw their savings and brought on the nation-wide bank closings. Those were days when everyone knew paralyzing fears.

History will record the fact that these fears were met, not by conquest, not by drawing on the moral resources and inner fortitude of the American citizen, but by a collection of wholesale materialistic schemes. These schemes included such devices as inflating the dollar, raising prices, expanding the government debt, paying farmers not to produce crops, government housing projects, and many others. The fears of unemployment and poverty in old age were to be eliminated wholesale through a planned economy, a new social order. By an elaborate system of book-keeping called Social Security, a whole nation was to win freedom from want and freedom from fear.

But while we were building our smug little house of Social Security, the whole world was crashing around us. Instead of achieving local security we find ourselves now in the midst of world-wide insecurity. Far from having eliminated the economic causes of fear, we now find these causes multiplied many times. To the fear of losing our money is now added the fear of losing our sons. To the fear of losing our jobs is added the fear of losing our lives. To the fear of depression and inflation is added the fear of losing the very freedoms for which the war is being fought.

At last we see, or are on the point of seeing, that materialism breeds worse fears than it cures; that economics and sociology create more social problems than they solve; that science makes it possible to destroy wealth and lives much faster than it can build them. It took years of science to achieve the airplane and to eliminate people's fear of flying. Now, suddenly, the airplane has become the greatest source of destruction and of fear on the globe. Cities which were decades in the building are blasted out of being in a night. Millions of people must regulate their lives in fear of these dread visitors.

This is the background against which the conquest of fear presents its philosophy of courage and of hope. It is a philosophy diametrically opposed to the dominant beliefs and practices of our materialistic age. One hesitates to use the words spiritual and moral because they have become catch words. Nevertheless, King's philosophy is a spiritual and a moral one, and the reader will gain from it a clearer concept of what these words really mean.

When I remember my reactions to the first portion of this book, I can readily picture the impatience and even scorn of many intellectuals and pseudo-intellectuals. Because of its emphasis on the religious nature of the universe and on the spiritual power of the individual, it may seem to them naïve. Because of its consistent condemnation of Mammon, of materialism and the economic-sociological interpretation of life, it may seem to them old-fashioned. Actually, the book is highly sophisticated and is more novel to-day than the day it was written because since that time we have strayed twenty years further from the truth.

One day I was having luncheon with a man who, during the course of the conversation, remarked: "I want to tell you how much I enjoyed your latest book,—" As almost any writer would, I pricked up my ears expectantly.

"Yes," he went on, "I got a great deal out of your recent book, but the book which helped me more than any I have ever read is a book called The Conquest of Fear, by Basil King. Do you happen to know it?"

"Know it!" I exclaimed. "I not only know it, I am just on the point of writing an introduction to a new edition of the book. Would you mind telling me how it helped you?"

He thereupon related how, at a certain period of his life, he had left an excellent position to take a new one which seemed more promising. It soon developed that the difficulties of this position were such as to make his success seem almost hopeless. He became obsessed with the idea that the people with whom he had to deal were "out to get him." His fears of the job and of his associates grew to the point where a nervous breakdown seemed inevitable.

One day his daughter told him that she needed a book in her school work which he remembered having packed in a box that had been stored in the attic and not yet opened. When he opened the box, the first book which he picked up was The Conquest of Fear. It was evidently one of those books which had somehow come into the possession of his family, but which he had never read.

This time, however, he sat down in the attic and began to read it. During the course of the next year or so he read it carefully not once but four or five times. "It marked the turning point in my life," he told me. "It enabled me to conquer the fears which were threatening to ruin me at the time, and it gave me a philosophy which has stood me in good stead ever since."

A philosophy which marked the turning point in his life and which has stood him in good stead ever since! The Conquest of Fear offers such a philosophy not only to individuals suffering from fears peculiar to them, but to a world of individuals suffering, or about to suffer, from the collapse of world-wide materialism. In this day of chaos and uncertainty, here is the modern version of the parable of the man who built his house upon a rock instead of on the sand: "and the rain descended, and the floods came, and the winds blew, and beat upon that house; and it fell not for it was founded upon a rock."

by Henry C. Link, Ph.D.

Fear And The Life-Principle

When I say that during most of my conscious life I have been a prey to fears I take it for granted that I am expressing the case of the majority of people. I cannot remember the time when a dread of one kind or another was not in the air. In childhood it was the fear of going to bed, of that mysterious time when regular life was still going on downstairs, while I was buried alive under sheets and blankets. Later it was the fear of school, the first contact of the tender little soul with life's crudeness. Later still there was the experience which all of us know of waking in the morning with a feeling of dismay at what we have to do on getting up; the obvious duties in which perhaps we have grown stale; the things we have neglected; those in which we have made mistakes; those as to which we have wilfully done wrong; those which weary or bore or annoy or discourage us. Sometimes there are more serious things still: bereavements, or frightfully adverse conditions, or hardships we never expected brought on us by someone else.

It is unnecessary to catalogue these situations, since we all at times in our lives have to face them daily. Fear dogs one of us in one way and another in another, but everyone in some way.

Look at the people you run up against in the course of a few hours. Everyone is living or working in fear. The mother is afraid for her children. The father is afraid for his business. The clerk is afraid for his job. The worker is afraid of his boss or his competitor. There is hardly a man who is not afraid that some other man will do him a bad turn. There is hardly a woman who is not afraid that things she craves may be denied her, or that what she loves may be snatched away. There is not a home or an office or a factory or a school or a church in which some hang-dog apprehension is not eating at the hearts of the men, women, and children who go in and out. I am ready to guess that all the miseries wrought by sin and sickness put together would not equal those we bring on ourselves by the means which perhaps we do least to counteract. We are not sick all the time; we are not sinning all the time; but all the time all of us—or practically all of us—are afraid of someone or something. If, therefore, one has the feeblest contribution to make to the defeat of such a foe it becomes difficult to withhold it.

But even with a view to conquering fear I should not presume to offer to others ideas worked out purely for myself had I not been so invited. I do not affirm that I have conquered fear, but only that in self-defence I have been obliged to do something in that direction. I take it for granted that what goes in that direction will go all the way if pursued with perseverance and good will. Having thus made some simple experiments—chiefly mental—with what to me are effective results, I can hardly refuse to tell what they have been when others are so good as to ask me.

And in making this attempt I must write from my own experience. No other method would be worth while. The mere exposition of a thesis would have little or no value. It is a case in which nothing can be helpful to others which has not been demonstrated for oneself, even though the demonstration be but partial.

In writing from my own experience I must ask the reader's pardon if I seem egoistic or autobiographical. Without taking oneself too smugly or too seriously one finds it the only way of reproducing the thing that has happened in one's own life and which one actually knows.

And when I speak above of ideas worked out purely for myself I do not, of course, mean that these ideas are original with me. All I have done has been to put ideas through the mill of my own mind, co-ordinating them to suit my own needs. The ideas themselves come from many sources. Some of these sources are, so deep in the past that I could no longer trace them; some are so recent that I know the day and hour when they revealed themselves, like brooks in the way. It would be possible to say to the reader, "I owe this to such and such a teaching, and that to such and such a man," only that references of the kind would be tedious. I fall back on what Emerson says: "Thought is the property of him who can entertain it; and of him who can adequately place it. A certain awkwardness marks the use of borrowed thoughts; but, as soon as we have learned what to do with them, they become our own. Thus all originality is relative." The thoughts that I shall express are my own to the extent that I have lived them—or tried to live them—though the wind that bloweth where it listeth may have brought them to my mind.

Nor do I think for a moment that what I have found helpful to me must of necessity be helpful to everyone. It may be helpful to someone. That is the limit of my hope. It is simple fact that no one can greatly help anyone else. The utmost we can do is to throw out an idea here and there which another may seize, and by which he may help himself. Borrowed help has the awkwardness which Emerson attributes to borrowed thoughts. It is only when a concept has lain for a time in a man's being, germinated there, and sprung into active life, that it is of much use to him; but by that time it has become his own. The kingdom of heaven must begin within oneself or we shall probably not find it anywhere.

These pages will contain, then, no recipe for the conquest of fear; they will offer, with much misgiving and diffidence, no more than the record of what one individual has done toward conquering it. This record is presented merely for what it is worth. It may be worth nothing. On the other hand, someone may find it worth something, and in that case all that the writer hopes for will be attained.

III

As a matter of fact, in my own case the reaction against fear was from the beginning more or less instinctive. With the first exercise of the reasoning faculty I tried to argue against the emotion. I remember that as a little boy I was afraid of a certain dog that barked at me when I went to a certain house to which I was sent perhaps two or three times a week. The house had a driveway, and from the minute of passing the entrance my knees trembled under me. But even then, I recall, it seemed to me that this terror was an incongruous thing in life, that it had no rightful place there, and that, if the world was what my elders told me it was, there must be in it a law of peace and harmony which as yet I hadn't arrived at. I cannot say that when the dog barked this reasoning did more than nerve me to drag my quaking limbs up to the doorstep, whence my enemy, a Skye terrier, invariably took flight.

During a somewhat stormy childhood and boyhood, in which there was a good deal of emotional stress, I never got beyond this point. Specific troubles were not few, and by the time I reached early manhood a habit of looking for them had been established. "What's it going to be now?" became a formula of anticipation before every new event. New events presented themselves most frequently as menaces. Hopes rarely loomed up without accompanying probabilities of disappointment. One adopted the plan of "expecting disappointment" as a means of cheating the "jinx." I am not painting my early life as any darker than most lives. It was, I fancy, as bright as the average life of youth.

IV

But, contrary to what is generally held, I venture to think that youth is not a specially happy period. Because young people rarely voice their troubles we are likely to think them serene and unafraid. That has not been my experience either with them or of them. While it is true that cares of a certain type increase with age the knowledge of how to deal with them increases, or ought to increase, in the same progression. With no practical experience to support them the young are up against the unknown and problematical—occupation, marriage, sexual urge, life in general—around which clings that terror of the dark which frightened them in childhood. Home training, school training, college training, religious training, social influences of every kind, throw the emphasis on dangers rather than on securities, so that the young life emerges into a haunted world. Some are reckless of these dangers, some grow hardened to them, some enjoy the tussle with them, some turn their minds away from them, while others, chiefly the imaginative or the intellectual, shrink from them with the discomfort which, as years go on, becomes worry, anxiety, foreboding, or any other of the many forms of care.

V

My own life followed what I assume to be the usual course, though in saying this I am anxious not to give an exaggerated impression. It was the usual course, not an unusual one. "There's always something" came to be a common mental phrase, and the something was, as a rule, not cheering. Neither, as a rule, was it terrible. It was just something—a sense of the carking hanging over life, and now and then turning to a real mischance or a heartache.

It strikes me as strange, on looking back, that so little attempt was made to combat fear by religion. In fact, as far as I know, little attempt was made to combat fear in any way. One's attention was not called to it otherwise than as a wholly inevitable state. You were born subject to fear as you were born subject to death, and that was an end of it.

Brought up in an atmosphere in which religion was our main preoccupation, I cannot recall ever hearing it appealed to as a counteragent to this most persistent enemy of man. In dealing with your daily dreads you simply counted God out. Either He had nothing to do with them or He brought them upon you. In any case His intervention on your behalf was not supposed to be in this world, and to look for rewards from Him here and now was considered a form of impiety. You were to be willing to serve God for naught; after which unexpected favours might be accorded you, but you were to hope for nothing as a right. I do not say that this is what I was taught; it was what I understood; but to the best of my memory it was the general understanding round about me. In my fight against fear, in as far as I made one, God was for many years of no help to me, or of no help of which I was aware. I shall return to the point later in telling how I came to "discover God" for myself, but not quite the same God, or not quite the same concept of God, which my youthful mind had supposed to be the only one.

VI

At the same time it was to a small detail in my religious training—or to be more exact in the explanation of the Bible given me as a boy—that I harked back when it became plain to me that either I must conquer fear or fear must conquer me. Having fallen into my mind like a seed, it lay for well on to thirty years with no sign of germination, till that "need," of which I shall have more to say presently, called it into life.

Let me state in a few words how the need made itself pressing.

It was, as life goes, a tolerably dark hour. I was on the borderland between young manhood and early middle age. For some years I had been losing my sight, on top of which came one of those troubles with the thyroid gland which medical science still finds obscure. For reasons which I need not go into I was spending an autumn at Versailles in France, unoccupied and alone.

If you know Versailles you know that it combines all that civilisation has to offer of beauty, magnificence, and mournfulness. A day's visit from Paris will give you an inkling of this, but only an inkling. To get it all you must live there, to be interpenetrated by its glory of decay. It is always the autumn of the spirit at Versailles, even in summer, even in spring; but in the autumn of the year the autumnal emotion of the soul is poignant beyond expression. Sad gardens stretch into sad parks; sad parks into storied and haunting forests. Long avenues lead to forgotten châteaux mellowing into ruin. Ghostly white statues astonish you far in the depths of woods where the wild things are now the most frequent visitors. A Temple of Love—pillared, Corinthian, lovely—lost in a glade to which lovers have probably not come in a hundred years—will remind you that there were once happy people where now the friendliest sound is that of the wood-chopper's axe or the horn of some far-away hunt. All the old tales of passion, ambition, feud, hatred, violence, lust, and intrigue are softened here to an aching sense of pity. At night you will hear the castle clock, which is said never once to have failed to strike the hour since Louis the Fourteenth put it in its place, tolling away your life as it has tolled away epochs.

Amid these surroundings a man ill, lonely, threatened with blindness, can easily feel what I may call the spiritual challenge of the ages. He must either be strong and rule; or he must be weak and go down. He must get the dominion over circumstance, or circumstance must get the dominion over him. To be merely knocked about by fate and submit to it, even in the case of seemingly inevitable physical infirmity, began to strike me as unworthy of a man.

It is one thing, however, to feel the impulse to get up and do something, and another to see what you can get up and do. For a time the spectre of fear had me in its power. The physical facts couldn't be denied, and beyond the physical facts

I could discern nothing. It was conceivable that one might react against a mental condition; but to react against a mysterious malady coupled with possibly approaching blindness was hardly to be thought of. When one added one's incapacity to work and earn a living, with all that that implies, it seemed as if it would take the faith that moves mountains to throw off the weight oppressing me. It is true that to move mountains you only need faith as a grain of mustard seed, but as far as one can judge not many of us have that much.

It was then that my mind went back all of a sudden to the kernel planted so many years before, in my island home, in the Gulf of St. Lawrence. If I become prolix over this it is only that I want to show how often it happens to parents, teachers, and others who deal with children, to throw out a thought which after lying dormant for years will become a factor in the life. Had it not been for the few words spoken then I should not, as far as I can see, now have such mastery over self as I have since attained—not very much—but I should not be writing these lines.

VII

My boyhood was placed in the times when Darwin's "Origin of Species" and "Descent of Man" had thrown the scientific and religious worlds into convulsion. The struggle between the old ideas and the new calls for no more than a reference here; but the teacher to whom I owe most was one who, while valuing the old, saw only an enrichment in the new, explaining the Bible in that spirit. So it happened that he spoke one day of the extraordinary ingenuity of the life-principle, which somehow came to the earth, in adapting itself to perpetually new conditions.

Nothing defeated it. For millions of years it was threatened by climatic changes, by the lack of food, by the ferocity of fellow-creatures. Heat, cold, flood, drought, earthquake, and volcanic eruption were forever against it. Struggling from stage to stage upward from the slime a new danger was always to it a new incentive to finding a new resource.

Pursued through the water it sought the land. Pursued on the land it sought the air. Pursued in the air it developed fleetness of wing, and in fleetness of wing a capacity for soaring, circling, balancing, dipping, and swinging on itself of which the grace must not blind us to the marvellous power of invention.

In other words, the impulses leading to the origin of species proclaim a resourcefulness on the part of what we call life which we have every reason to think inexhaustible. Whatever the Fount of Being from which the life-principle first came into the waters of our earth there is no question but that with it came a conquest-principle as well. Had it been possible to exterminate the life-principle it would never have gone further than the age which saw the extinction of the great reptiles. The great reptiles went, but the life-principle stayed on, with the ability to assume, within our limited observation, all the forms between the bacillus and the elephant, while as to what lies beyond our observation the possibilities are infinite.

Long before it works up to man we see this amazing force stemming an uncountable number of attacks, and meeting ruinous conditions with daring contrivances. For one kind of danger it develops a shell, for another a sting, for another a poison, for another a protective colouration. To breathe in the sea it puts forth gills, and makes lungs for itself when stranded on the land. In glacial cold it finds the means of growing fur; when heat and cold assail it by turns it packs itself with feathers; when climates become temperate it produces hair. For the creature which keeps to the water it webs the foot; for that which takes to the trees it makes the toes prehensile; for the one which learns to stand erect and run along the ground it flattens the sole, making it steady and supporting. To resist, to survive, to win through, is the end to which the life-principle sets itself with such singleness of aim as to unfold a wealth of potentiality astounding to us in looking backward.

VIII

This was the idea which came back to me that autumn at Versailles, and from which in the course of time I drew my conclusions.

Briefly, those conclusions were to the effect that as individuals we need difficulties to overcome, and that fear is a stimulus to overcoming them. Otherwise expressed, fear loses much of its fearfulness when we see it as the summons to putting forth new energies. Unless we were conscious of the energies such a call would not reach us. The creatures preceding man could have felt no misgiving, since they lacked the imagination essential to a dread. Such fear as they were equal to must have seized them in paroxysms of terror when calamities threatened to overwhelm them. If they made good their escape no trace of the fear remained behind, the brain having little or no power of retention. We may take it for granted that the pterodactyl and the trachodon had none of the foreboding based on experience which destroys the peace of man.

Fear, as we understand it, was in itself a signal of advance. It could only have begun with the exercise of reason. Arrived at the rudiments of memory the creature must have been able to perceive, however dimly, that the thing which had happened might happen again. Adding the first stirrings of imagination he must have constructed possible events in which the danger would come from the same causes as before. With the faculties to remember, to reason, and to imagine all at work we reach the first stages of man.

Man was born into fear in that he was born into a world of which most of the energies were set against him. He was a lone thing fighting his own battle. The instinct for association which made the mammals different from other animals didn't help him much, since association did not bring mutual help as a matter of course, and never has done so. A man could count on no one but himself. Not only were prodigious natural forces always menacing him with destruction; not only was the beast his enemy and he the enemy of the beast; but his hand was against his fellow-man and his fellow-man's hand against him. This mutual hostility followed men in their first groupings into communities, and only to a degree have we lived it down in the twentieth century.

Perhaps this conviction that a man's strength lay in standing single-handed against circumstance was the first small discovery I made in my own fight with fear. Looking back on the developments which had brought man into the world I saw a marvellous power of getting round difficulties when you couldn't cut through them. Just as a river which cannot flow over a rock can glide about its feet and turn it into a picturesque promontory, so I recognised in myself an inborn human faculty for "sidestepping" that which blocked my way, when I couldn't break it down.

I left Versailles with just that much to the good—a perception that the ages had bequeathed me a store of abilities which I was allowing to lie latent. Moving into Paris, to more cheerful surroundings, I took up again the writing of the book I had abandoned more than a year previously. After long seclusion I began to see a few people, finding them responsive and welcoming. My object in stating these unimportant details is merely to show that in proportion as I ceased to show fear the life-principle hastened to my aid. Little by little I came to the belief that the world about me was a system of co-operative friendliness, and that it was my part to use it in that way.

IX

To use it in that way was not easy. I was so accustomed to the thought of Nature as a complex of self-seeking cruelties, the strong preying on the weak, and the weak defenceless, that the mere idea of its containing a ruling co-operative principle seemed at times far-fetched. To the common opinion of the day, my own included, the conception of a universe that would come to a man's aid the minute a man came to his own was too much like a fairy tale. It may indeed be a fairy tale. All I know is that in my own case it is the way in which it seems to have worked. I think I have caught a glimpse of a constructive use for that which I had previously thought of as only destructive and terrible.

This is what I mean. The life-principle having, through unknown millions of years, developed the conquest-principle by meeting difficulties and overcoming them, the difficulties had a value. To man, especially, the menace of Nature, the ferocity of the beast, and the enmity of his fellow-man furnished the incentive to his upward climb. Had all been easy he would have stayed where he was. He would never have called mental powers to his physical aid, nor appealed to spiritual faculties when the mental fell short of his requirements. Spurred on by a necessity which grew more urgent in proportion as the life-principle widened its scope, the conquest-principle became an impulse which would brook no denying. Man grew by it; but the fact remains that he would not have grown had there been nothing for him to struggle with.

To me it seems basic to the getting rid of fear to know that our trials, of whatever nature, are not motiveless. In our present stage of development we could hardly do without them. So often looking like mere ugly excrescences on life they are in reality the branches by which we catch on and climb. They are not obstacles to happiness for the reason that the only satisfying happiness we are equal to as yet is that of wrestling with the difficult and overcoming it. Every call of duty has its place in this ideal; every irksome job, every wearisome responsibility. The fact that we are not always aware of it in no way annuls the other fact that it is so. Boredom, monotony, drudgery, bereavement, loneliness, all the clamour of unsatisfied ambitions and aching sensibilities, have their share in this divine yearning of the spirit to grasp what as yet is beyond its reach. All of that hacking of the man to fit the job rather than the shaping of the job to fit the man, which is, I imagine, the source of most of the discontent on earth, has its place here, as well as the hundreds of things we shouldn't do if we were not compelled to. Whatever summons us to conflict summons us to life, and life, as we learn from a glance at the past, never shirks the challenge.

It never shirks the challenge, and, what is more, it never fails to find the expedient by which the new demand is to be satisfied. To the conquest of fear that plank must be foundational. As far as we can learn there never was an emergency yet which the life-principle was not equipped to meet. When all existing methods had been used up it invented new ones; when seemingly at the end of its new resources it was only beginning to go on again.

X

The deduction I make is this, that a law which was operative on such a scale before man had come into the world at all must be still more effective now that we can help to carry it out. The life-principle is not less ingenious than it ever was, while the conquest-principle must have widely expanded. It is an axiom in all progress that the more we conquer the more easily we conquer. We form a habit of conquering as insistent as any other habit. Victory becomes, to some degree, a state of mind. Knowing ourselves superior to the anxieties, troubles, and worries which obsess us, we are superior. It is a question of attitude in confronting them. It is more mental than it is material. To be in harmony with the life-principle and the conquest-principle is to be in harmony with power; and to be in harmony with power is to be strong as a matter of course.

The individual is thus at liberty to say: "The force which never failed before is not likely to fail in my case. The fertility of resource which circumvented every kind of obstacle to make me what I am—a vertebrate, breathing, walking, thinking entity, capable of some creative expression of my own—will probably not fall short now that I have immediate use for it. Of what I get from the past, prehistoric and historic, perhaps the most subtle distillation is the fact that so far is the life-principle from balking at need, need is essential to its activity. Where there is no need it seems to be quiescent; where there is something to be met, contended with, and overcome, it is furiously 'on the job.' That life-principle is my principle. It is the seed from which I spring. It is my blood, my breath, my brain. I cannot cut myself off from it; it cannot cut itself off from me. Having formed the mastodon to meet one set of needs and the butterfly to meet another, it will form, something to meet mine, even if something altogether new. The new—or what seems new to me—is apparently the medium in which it is most at home. It repeats itself never—not in two rosebuds, not in two snowflakes. Who am I that I should be overlooked by it, or miss being made the expression of its infinite energies?"

XI

What this reasoning did for me from the start was to give me a new attitude toward the multifold activity we call life. I saw it as containing a principle that would work with me if I could work with it. My working with it was the main point, since it was working with me always. Exactly what that principle was I could not at the time have said; I merely recognised it as being there.

The method of working with it was simple in idea, however difficult in practice. It was a question of my own orientation. I had to get mentally into harmony with the people and conditions I found about me. I was not to distrust them; still less was I to run away from them. I was to make a parable of my childish experience with the Skye terrier, assuming that life was organised to do me good. I remembered how many times the Bible begins some bit of pleading or injunction with the words, "Fear not." Other similar appeals came back to me. "Say to them that are of a fearful heart, Be strong I fear not."[1] "Quit yourselves like men; be strong."[2] "O man greatly beloved, fear not! Peace be unto thee! Be strong, yea, be Strong."[3] When, at some occasional test, dismay or self-pity took hold of me I formed a habit of saying to myself, in our expressive American idiom: "This is your special stunt. It's up to you to do this thing just as if you had all the facilities. Go at it boldly, and you'll find unexpected forces closing round you and Coming to your aid."

Which is just what I did find. To an amazing degree people were friendly, while conditions became easier. Fear diminished because I had fewer things to be afraid of. Having fewer things to be afraid of my mind was clearer for work. Work becoming not only more of a resource but more remunerative as well, all life grew brighter. Fear was not overcome; I had only made a more or less hesitating stand against it; but even from doing that I got positive results.

The Life-Principle And God

I

It is obvious that one could not dwell much on the power of the life-principle without coming sooner or later to the thought of God. As already hinted, I did not come to it at once because my conception of God made Him of so little use to me.

And yet, in popular phraseology, I had "served" God all my life. That is, brought up in an atmosphere in which the Church was a divinely instituted system for utilising God, I served the system, without getting much beyond the surface plane of what were technically known as "services." When trial came such services offered me an anodyne, but not a cure.

II

The first suggestion, that my concept of God might not be sufficient to my needs came out of a conversation in New York. It was with a lady whom I met but that once, within a year or two after my experience at Versailles. I have forgotten how we chanced on the subject, but I remember that she asked me these questions:

"When you think of God how do you think of Him? How do you picture Him? What does He seem like?"

Trying to reply I recognised a certain naivete, a certain childishness, in my words even as I uttered them. In my thoughts I saw God as three supernal men, seated on three supernal thrones, enshrined in some vague celestial portion of space which I denominated Heaven. Between Him and me there was an incalculable distance which He could bridge but I could not. Always He had me at the disadvantage that He saw what I did, heard what I said, read what I thought, punishing me for everything amiss, while I could reach Him only by the uncertain telephony of what I understood as prayer. Even then my telephone worked imperfectly. Either the help I implored wasn't good for me, or my voice couldn't soar to His throne.

The lady smiled, but said nothing. The smile was significant. It made me feel that a God who was no more than what I had described could hardly be the Universal Father, and set me to thinking on my own account.

III

I wish it were possible to speak of God without the implication of dealing with religion. By this I mean that I am anxious to keep religion out of this whole subject of the conquest of fear. The minute you touch on religion, as commonly understood, you reach the sectarian. The minute you reach the sectarian you start enmities. The minute you start enmities you get mental discords. And the minute you get mental discords no stand against fear is possible.

But I mean a little more than this. Man, as at present developed, has shown that he hardly knows what to do with religion, or where to put it in his life. This is especially true of the Caucasian, the least spiritually intelligent of all the great types of our race. Fundamentally the white man is hostile to religion. He attacks it as a bull a red cloak, goring it, stamping on it, tearing it to shreds. With the Caucasian as he is this fury is instinctive. Recognising religion as the foe of the materialistic ideal he has made his own he does his best to render it ineffective.

Of this we need no better illustration than the state of what we conventionally know as Christendom. Christendom as we see it is a purely Caucasian phase of man's struggle upward, with Caucasian merits and Caucasian defects. Nowhere is its defectiveness more visible than in what the Caucasian has made of the teaching of Jesus Christ. It was probably a misfortune for the world that almost from the beginning that teaching passed into Caucasian guardianship. I see in the New Testament no indication on the part of Our Lord and the Apostles of wishing to separate themselves from Semitic co-operation. The former taught daily in the Temple; the latter, as they went about the world, made the synagogue the base of all their missions. The responsibility for the breach is not under discussion here. It is enough to note that it took place, and that Caucasian materialism was thus deprived of a counteragent in Hebrew spiritual wisdom. Had this corrective maintained its place it is possible that religion might now be a pervasive element in the Caucasian's life instead of being pigeon-holed.

IV

The Caucasian pigeon-holes God. Otherwise expressed, he keeps God in a specially labelled compartment of life, to be brought out for occasional use, and put back when the need is over. It is difficult to mention God to a Caucasian reader without inducing an artificial frame of mind. As there are people who put on for strangers and guests an affected, unnatural politeness different from their usual breezy spontaneity, so the Caucasian assumes at the thought of God a mental habit which can only be described as sanctimonious. God is not natural to the Caucasian; the Caucasian is not natural with God. The mere concept takes him into regions in which he feels uneasy. He may call his uneasiness reserve or reverence, or by some other dignified name; but at bottom it is neither more nor less than uneasiness. To minimise this distress he relegates God to special days, to special hours, to services and ceremonials. He can thus wear and bear his uncomfortable cloak of gravity for special times, after which he can be himself again. To appeal to God otherwise than according to the tacitly accepted protocol is to the average Caucasian either annoying or in bad form.

I should like, then, to dissociate the thought of God from the artificial, sanctimonious, preternaturally solemn connotations which the Name is certain to bring up. I want to speak of Him with the same kind of ease as of the life-principle. I repeat, that I never found Him of much use in allaying fear till I released Him from the Caucasian pigeon-hole to see Him, as it were, in the open. Once in the open I got rid, to some degree, of the Caucasian limitations of thinking along the lines of sect, just as in the infinitude of the air you can forget for a minute houses with rooms and walls. The discovery—that is, discovery for myself—that God is Universal, which is not so obvious as it sounds, was, I think, the first great step I made in finding that within that Universal fear should be impossible.

V

About the same time I chanced on a passage written by Joseph Joubert, an eighteenth-century French Catholic, not so well known to the modern reader as he ought to be, which impressed me deeply.

"L'âme ne peut se mouvoir, s'éveiller, ouvrir les yeux, sans santir Dieu. On sent Dieu avec l'âme comme on sent l'air avec le corps. Oseraije le dire? On connaît Dieu facilement pourvu qu'on ne se contraigne pas à le definir—The soul cannot move, wake, or open the eyes without perceiving God. We perceive God through the soul as we feel air on the body. Dare I say it? We can know God easily so long as we do not feel it necessary to define Him."

I began to see that, like most Caucasian Christians, I had been laying too much stress on the definition. The Trinity had, so to speak, come between me and the Godhead. I had, unconsciously, attached more importance to God's being Three than to His being God. Seeing Him as Three I instinctively saw Him as Three Persons. Seeing Him as Three Persons I did not reflect that the word Person as applied to God must be used in a sense wholly different from that in which we employ it with regard to men. To get into what I call the open I had to bring myself to understand that we cannot enclose the Infinite in a shape, or three shapes, resembling in any way the being with digestive organs, arms, and legs, which worked its way up from slime.

That is, in order to "dwell in the secret place of the Most High,"[4] where one is immune from fear, I was obliged to give up the habit of embodying God in any form. I had to confess that what is meant by the Three Persons in One God

I did not know. Furthermore, I saw no necessity for thinking that I knew, since such knowledge must transcend all scope of the human mind. The formula, if you must have a formula, is one thing; but the turning it into a statute of limitations and applying it to the Illimitable is another.

To make my position clearer, and to avoid the subject of religion, let me add that, inferring from the Bible that there is a Father, a Son, and a Holy Ghost, I did not feel it imperative on my part to go beyond this use of terms. Merely to abstain from definition was like a load taken off my mind. How the Son was begotten of the Father, or the Holy Ghost proceeded from them both, or what eternal mysteries were symbolised in this purely human phraseology, were, it seemed to me, matters with which I need not concern myself, seeing that they passed all my comprehension. Not the Trinity should come first to powers so limited as mine—but God.

It dawned on me, too, that God need not necessarily be to me what He is to others, nor to others what He is to me. Of the Infinite the finite mind can only catch a finite glimpse. I see what I can see; another sees what he can see. The visions may be different, and yet each vision may be true. Just as two painters painting the same landscape will give dissimilar views of it, so two minds contemplating God will take of Him only what each is fitted to receive. Water poured into differently coloured glasses will take on the colour of the cup which it fills, even though it be the self-same water in them all. If I find God for myself I shall probably not behold in Him exactly what anyone else in the whole world or in all time has ever beheld in Him before.

I saw, too, that from a certain point of view the stand of the agnostic is a right one. We cannot know God in the sense of knowing His being or His "Personality," any more than we can know the essence of the life-principle. Just as we know the life-principle only from what it does, so we know God only from such manifestations of Himself as reach our observation. Everything else is inference. Because we see something of His goodness we infer that He is good; because we experience something of His love we infer that He is loving; because we behold something of His power we infer that He is almighty. It is first of all a matter of drawing our conclusions, and then of making those conclusions the food of the inner spiritual man whose life is independent of the mortal heart and brain. But a sense in which God is "unknowable" to us has to be admitted.

I make this statement now in order not to be misunderstood when later I may say that God must be this or that. Though I shall do so for the sake of brevity it will always be in the sense that, if God is what we have inferred from His manifestations, He must be this or that. In other words, having to some degree worked my own way out of fear I must tell how I came to feel that I know the Unknowable, doing it with the inexact phraseology which is all I find to hand.

VI

Reaching the conclusions noted above I was relieved of the pressure of traditions and instructions. Traditions and instructions helped me in that they built the ship in which I was to put to sea. The discoveries had to be my own. The God of whom I had heard at my mother's knee, as the phrase goes, had always been shadowy to me; the God who was served by "services" had always seemed remote. A God who should be "my God," as the psalmists say so often, must, I felt, be found by me myself, through living, searching, suffering, and struggling onward a step or two at a time. "That's pretty near free-thinking, isn't it?" a clergyman, to whom I tried to explain myself, once said to me. "No," I replied; "but it is pretty near thinking free."

To think freely about God became a first necessity; to think simply a second one. The Universal Father had been almost lost to me behind veil after veil of complexities. The approaches to Him seemed to have been made so roundabout, requiring so many intermediaries. Long before I had dared to think of what I may call emancipation, the "scheme of salvation," as it was termed, had struck me as an excessively complicated system of machinery, considering the millions upon millions who had need of it. In theory you were told, according to St. Paul, to "come boldly before the throne of the heavenly grace," but in practice you were expected to do it timidly.

You were expected to do it timidly because the pigeon-holed Caucasian God was represented—unconsciously perhaps—as difficult, ungenial, easily offended. He measured your blindness and weakness by the standard of His own knowledge and almightiness. A puritan God, extremely preoccupied with morals as some people saw them, He was lenient, apparently, to the narrow-minded, the bitter of tongue, and the intolerant in heart. He was not generous. He was merciful only when you paid for His mercy in advance. To a not inconsiderable degree He was the hard Caucasian business man, of whom He was the reflection, only glorified and crowned.

It will be evident, of course, that I am not speaking of "the Father" of the New Testament, nor of the official teaching of any church or theology. To the rank and file of Caucasians "the Father" of the New Testament is very little known, while the official teaching of churches and theologies is so hard to explain that not much of it gets over to the masses of those willing to subscribe to it. I refer only to the impression on the mind of the man in the street; and to the man in the street God, as he understands Him, is neither a very friendly nor a very comprehensible element in life. Instead of mitigating fear He adds to it, not in the Biblical sense of "fearing God," but in that of sheer animal distrust.

VII

While turning these things over in my mind I got some help from two of the words most currently in Christian use. I had long known that the English equivalents of the Latin equivalents of the terms the New Testament writers used gave but a distorted idea of the original sense; but I had let that knowledge lie fallow.

The first of these words was Repentance. In these syllables there is almost no hint of the idea which fell from the evangelistic pen, while the word has been soaked in emotional and sentimental associations it was never intended to be mixed with. The Metanoia; which painted a sober, reflective turning of the mind, had been so overcharged with the dramatic that sober, reflective people could hardly use the expression any more. Repentance had come to have so strong a gloss of the hysterical as to be almost discredited by men of common sense. It was a relief, therefore, to remember that it implied no more than a turning to God by a process of thought; and that a process of thought would find Him.

The other word was Salvation. Here again our term of Latin derivation gives no more than the faintest impression of the beauty beyond beauty in that which the sacred writer used. Soteria—a Safe Return! That is all. Nothing complicated; nothing high-strung; nothing casuistical. Only a—Safe Return! Yet all human experience can be read into the little phrase, with all human liberty to wander—and come back. True, one son may never leave the Father's home, so that all that it contains is his; but there is no restraint on the other son from getting his knowledge as he will, even to the extent of becoming a prodigal. The essential is in the Safe Return, the Soteria, when the harlots and the husks have been tried and found wanting.

I do not exaggerate when I say that the simplicity of these conceptions was so refreshing as almost to give me a new life. One could say to God, with the psalmist, "Thou art my hiding place; thou shalt preserve me from trouble; thou shalt compass me about with songs of deliverance"—and mean it. One could conceive of it as possible to turn toward Him—and reach, the objective. The way was open; the access was free; the progress as rapid as thought could make it. One could think of oneself as knowing God, and be aware of no forcing of the note.

"We can know God easily so long as we do not feel it necessary to define Him." Once having grasped this truth I began to see how natural knowing God became. The difficulty of the forced, of the artificial, of the mere assent to what other people say, of which the Caucasian to his credit is always impatient, seemed by degrees to melt away from me. No longer defining God I no longer tried to know Him in senses obviously impossible. I ceased trying to imagine Him. Seeing Him as infinite, eternal, changeless, formless because transcending form, and indescribable because transcending words and thoughts, I could give myself up to finding Him in the ways in which He would naturally be revealed to me.

VIII

These, of course, were in His qualities and His works.

Let me speak of the latter first.

I think light was the medium through which I at once felt myself to be seeing God. By this I mean nothing pantheistic—not that the light was God—but God's first and most evident great sign. Then there was the restful darkness. There were the moon and the stars, "the hosts of heaven," as the Hebrews aptly called them, becoming more and more amazing as an expression of God the more we learn how to read them. Then there were the elements, the purifying wind, the fruitful rain, the exhilaration of snow-storms, the action and reaction from heat and cold. Then there was beauty: first, the beauty of the earth, of mountains, of seas, and all waters, of meadows, grainfields, orchards, gardens, and all growing things; then, the beauty of sound, from the soughing of the wind in the pines to the song of the hermit-thrush. There was the beauty wrought by man, music, painting, literature, and all art. There were the myriad forms of life. There were kindness and friendship and family affection and fun—but the time would fail me! God being the summing up of all good things, since all good things proceed from Him, must be seen by me in all good things it I am to see Him at all.

I had heard from childhood of a world in which God was seen, and of another world, this world, in which He was not seen. I came to the conclusion that there was no such fantastic, unnatural division in what we call creation—that there was only one world—the world in which God is seen. "The soul cannot move, wake, or open the eyes without perceiving God." It is a question of physical vision, with spiritual comprehension.

IX

Seeing God breaking through all that I had previously thought of as barriers, it was easy to begin to think of Him as Universal. I say begin to think, because God's Infinitude had been only a word to me hitherto, not a quality realised and felt. I do not presume to say that to any adequate degree I feel and realise it now;

but the habit of looking on every good thing as a sign of His activity cannot but bring Him close to me.

That is my chief point with regard to the Infinite—that it must be here. As I used to think of infinity I saw it stretching to boundless reaches away from me; but only from the point of view of present Good being present God did the value of the Infinite come to lie in its nearness rather than in its power of filling unimaginable space. On my part it was inverse mental action, seeking God where I was capable of finding Him, and not in regions I could never range.

But having grasped the fact that the Universal, wherever else it was, must be with me the purely abstract became a living influence. I felt this the more when to the concept of Infinitude I added that of Intelligence. I use the much-worked word intelligence because there is no other; but when one thinks for a second of what must be the understanding of an Infinite Mind, intelligence as a descriptive term becomes absurdly inadequate.

This was the next fact which, if I may so express myself, I made my own—that not only the Universal is ever with me, but that it is ever with me with ever-active concern. There was a time when it was hard for me to believe that a Mind busied with the immensities of the universe could come down to such trivial affairs as mine. Important as I might be to myself I could hardly be otherwise than lost amid the billions of forms of life which had come into existence through the ages. To the Three in One, on the Great White Throne, in the far-away Heaven, I must be a negligible thing, except when I forced myself on the divine attention. Even then it was hardly conceivable that, with whole solar systems to regulate, I could claim more than a passing glance from the all-seeing eye.

But to an Infinite Mind bathing me round and round I must be as much the object of regard as any solar system. To such a Mind nothing is small, no one thing farther from its scope than another. God could have no difficulty in attending to me, seeing that from the nature of His mental activity, to put it in that way, He could not lose sight of me nor let me go. When an object is immersed in water it gives no extra trouble to the water to close round it. It can't help doing it. The object may be as small as a grain of dust or as big as a warship; to the water it is all the same. Immersed in the Infinite Mind, closed round by it, it was giving God no extra trouble to think of me, of my work, my desires, the objects with which I was living, since by the nature of His Being He could do nothing else.

Having established it with myself that Universal Presence was also Universal Thought I had made another step toward the elimination of fear. I took still another when I added the truth of Universal Love.

I need hardly say that this progression was not of necessity in a strictly consecutive order, nor did it come by a process of reasoning out from point to point. I was simply the man in the street dealing with great ideas of which he had heard ever since he had been able to hear anything, but trying at last to see what they meant to him. My position might have been described in the words used by William James in one of his Letters to indicate his own. "The Divine, for my active life, is limited to abstract concepts, which, as ideals, interest and determine me, but do so but faintly, in comparison with what a feeling of God might effect, if I had one. It is largely a question of intensity, but differences of intensity may make the whole centre of one's energy shift." I did have a "feeling of God" however vague; but I had more of the feeling of a Church. I could dimly discern the Way, without going on to the Truth and the Life which give the Way its value. It will be evident then that if my "discoveries" along these lines were discoveries in the obvious, it was in that obvious to which we mortals so often remain blind.

During many years the expression, the love of God, was to me like a winter sunshine, bright without yielding warmth. I liked the words; I knew they expressed a truth; but between me and the truth there was the same kind of distance which I felt to lie between myself and God. "It is largely a question of intensity," to repeat what has just been quoted from William James, "but differences of intensity may make the whole centre of one's energy shift." My conception of the love of God lacked just that quality—intensity.

It came, to some degree, with the realisation that the Universal Thought must be with me. A non-loving Universal Thought was too monstrous a concept to entertain. The God who "broke through" my many misunderstandings with so much good and beauty could have only one predominating motive. The coming of my spiritual being to this planet might be a mystery wrapped in darkness, and yet I could not but believe that the Universal Father was behind that coming and that I was His son. I could rest my case there. The love of God, after having long been like a doctrinal tenet for which one had to strive, became reasonable, natural, something to be understood. Finding that love in so many places in which I had seen mere physical phenomena, and in so many lovely things I had never placed to its credit, I began to feel that life could be infused and transformed by it, in proportion as my own perception grew. So, little by little, the centre of energy shifted, as one came to understand what the Sons of Korah meant when they sang, "God is our refuge and strength, a very present help in trouble. Therefore will we not fear though the earth be removed, and though the mountains be carried into, the midst of the sea."[5] With Universal Thought concentrated in love upon oneself fear must be forced backward.

And especially when you add to that the concept of Almighty Power. This fourth and last of the great attributes is the one with which I, as an individual, have found it most difficult to clothe the Infinite. I mean that it is the one for which it is hardest for me to develop what William James calls "a feeling," an inner realisation. I lay no stress upon this. It is a question of growth. The Presence, the Thought, the Love have become to me what I may be permitted to call tremulously vivid. In proportion as they are vivid I get the "feeling" of Almightiness exercised on my behalf; in proportion as they are tremulous the Almightiness may remain in my consciousness, but it seems exercised on my behalf but slightly.

In other words, the Infinitude of Thought and Love are, to some extent, apprehended by my inner self, while the Infinitude of Power is as yet to me rather an intellectual abstraction. What my inner self may be I am not prepared to say, but I know that it is there, as everyone else knows that it is in him. "Strengthened with might by the Spirit in the inner man,"[6] is what St. Paul says, and I suppose most of us recognise the fact that our inner self is stronger or weaker in proportion as it is more nourished or less nourished by our sense of the Being of God. It is largely a question of intensity. If I interpret William James aright he means by "a feeling" an intellectual concept after it has passed beyond the preliminary keeping of the brain, and become the possession of that inner man which is the vital self. To this vital self the sense of Almighty Power really used for me is still, to a great degree, outside my range.

I make the confession not because it is of interest, but because it illustrates a main deduction which I should now like to draw. It is to the effect that God is with us to be utilised. His Power, His Love, His Thought, His Presence, must be at our disposal, like other great forces, such as sunshine and wind and rain. We can use them or not, as we please. That we could use them to their full potentiality is, of course, not to be thought of; but we can use them in proportion to our ability. If I, the individual, still lack many things; if I am still a prey to lingering fears; it is probably because I have not yet rooted out a stubborn disbelief in His Power. If I succeed in this I shall doubtless be able to seize more of His bounty. It is not a question of His giving, but of my capacity to take.

The contrary, I venture to think, is the point of view of most of us. We consider God somewhat as we do a wealthy man whom we know to be a miser, forming the shrewd surmise that we shall not get much out of him. The God who fails to protect us from fear fails, I believe, because we see Him first of all as a niggard God. He is a niggard not merely with regard to money but all the good things for which He has given us a desire, with no intention of allowing that desire to be gratified. Once more, He is the hard Caucasian business man, whom His subordinates serve because they don't see what else to do, but whom they rarely love.

We shall not, in my judgment, overcome fear till we see Him as He surely must be, generous beyond all our conceptions of generosity. Years, experience, many trials, and some knowledge of the world, have convinced me that we have no lawful or harmless cravings for which, as far as God is concerned, there is not abundant satisfaction. I am convinced that absolute confidence in God's overflowing liberality of every sort is essential to the conquest of fear. If we don't profit by that liberality the fault is not His but our own. I am tempted to think that the belief of so many generations of nominal Christians in a God whose power was chiefly shown in repressions, denials, and capricious disappointments is responsible, in so small measure, for our present world-distress.

In my own case it was a matter of re-education. To find God for myself I had to be willing to let some of my old cherished ideas go. They may have been true of God as He reveals Himself to others; they are not true of Him as He makes Himself known to me. The Way that leads me to the Truth and the Life is undoubtedly the Way I must follow.

Doing that I have found so much, mentally, emotionally, materially, which I never had before, that I cannot but look for more as my absorbing power increases. The process is akin to that of the unshrivelling of the inner man, as a bud will unfold when the sunshine becomes strong enough. The transformation must be in thought. There must be first the Metanoia, the change of mind, the new set of concepts; and then the Soteria, the Safe Return, to the high, sane ideal of a co-operative Universe, with a loving, lavish Universal Heart behind it.

"To the chief Musician for the Sons of Korah:

"'God is our refuge and strength, a very present help in trouble. Therefore will we not fear though the earth be removed, and though the mountains be carried into the midst of the sea.... Come, behold the works of the Lord.... He maketh wars to cease unto the end of the earth; he breaketh the bow, he cutteth the spear in sunder, he burneth the chariot in the fire.... Be still then, and know that I am God,'"[7]

God And His Self-Expression

I

It will be clear from what I have said already that I see no fundamental conquest of fear that is not based in God. There may be knacks by which fear can be nipped and expedients by which it may be outwitted, but its extermination can be brought about, it seems to me, only in one way. According to our capacity and our individual needs we must know God; and knowing God is not as difficult as the Caucasian mind is apt to think. It stands to reason that if knowing God, in the senses in which it is possible to know Him, is so essential to mankind it could not be difficult. The making it difficult is part of the dust the Caucasian throws in his own eyes.

We know God through His Self-Expression, and His Self-Expression is round about us in every form. Except through His Self-Expression there is no way of our knowing Him. No speculation or theory will teach us to know Him. It must be His own revelation of Himself, or nothing.

II

Such little knowledge of Him as has come to me came much more freely when I began to look for that revelation not alone in solemn mysteries, or through the mediumship of prophets, apostles, and ancient scriptures, but in the sights and sounds and happenings of every day. Here I must ask not to be misunderstood. The solemn mysteries have their place, but it is one of climax. The mediumship of prophets, apostles, and ancient scriptures is of unreckonable value, after I have done something for myself. By this I do not mean that all cannot work together simultaneously, but rather that it is useless for the soul to strike only at the more advanced, having ignored the elementary.

As I write I look out on a street full of the touches of spring. The rain-washed grass is of bright new green. The elms are in tenderest leaf, the hawthorn bursting into flower. Here and there a yellow clump of forsythia is like a spot of sunshine. Tulips are opening their variegated cups, and daffodils line the walls. Dogs are capering about, a collie, a setter, a Boston terrier. Birds are carrying straws or bits of string to weave into their nests—or singing—or flying—or perching on boughs. Children are playing—boys on bicycles eagerly racing nowhere—little girls with arms round each others' waists, prattling after their kind. Overhead is a sky of that peculiar blue for which the Chinese have a word which means "the blue of the sky after rain," a hue which only these masters in colour have, to my knowledge, specially observed.

How can I help seeing so much beauty and sweetness as the manifestation of God? How could He show Himself to me more smilingly? How can I talk of not seeing God when I see this? True, it may be no more than the tip of the fringe of the hem of the robe in which His Being is arrayed; but at least it must be that. True, also, that beautiful as these things appear to physical eyes they must be still more beautiful to spiritual eyes—the eyes of those who have passed on, for instance—to say nothing of the delight which God must have in them Himself. But even with my imperfect mortal vision they are rapturously good, a veritable glimpse of the Divine.

This is what I mean by the elementary—the common, primary thing, the thing I look at every day and hardly ever accredit to its source. I am not speaking pantheistically here, any more than when I spoke of light. These things are not God, or part of God. They are expressions of God. If I speak of seeing God in them I mean that in them, as well as in many other simple things, we see Him as nearly as is possible to such comprehension as ours. "No human eye," writes St. John, "has ever seen God: the only Son, who is in the Father's bosom—He has made Him known."[8] He made Him known in His own Person; but He appealed also to the everyday sights and sounds, the lily of the field, the blowing wind, the sparrow falling, the children at their mothers' knees, for the evidence to declare Him. As expressions of Him they may be misinterpreted by the error in my physical senses, or distorted by my limitations of spiritual perception; but even then they bring Him near to me in the kind of radiance which I can catch.

III

In order to banish fear I think it necessary to train the thought to seeing God as expressing Himself in all the good and pleasant and enjoyable things that come to us. This means forming a habit. It means saying to oneself daily, hourly, "This is God," "That is God," of incidents, persons, and things we have rarely thought of in that relation. To do this is not as easy as it would be if our race-mind worked that way; but unfortunately it does not. In general we take our good things for granted, complaining that they are not better. The things we lack are more vivid to us, as a rule, than those we have acquired. Having hung, as it were, a cloud about ourselves we disregard the uncountable ways in which God persists in shining through, in spite of our efforts to shut Him out.

To try to enumerate the uncountable would be folly. You cannot reckon the good which comes to every one of us through such channels as family, home, friendship, income, business, amusements, studies, holidays, journeys, sports, books, pictures, music, and the other hardly noticed pleasures of any single day. We are used to them. To ascribe them specially to God would seem to us far-fetched. That is, theoretically we may ascribe them to God, but practically we dissociate Him from them. Few of us, I think, ever pause to remember that through them He is making Himself known to us before doing it in any other way.

And yet, it seems to me, this is the beginning of our recognition of the Divine. I have little hesitation in saying that this is what parents should teach children before they teach them to lisp prayers. The prayers have hardly any meaning to the baby-mind, and not much more than a sentimental influence on the later life, if they have as much as that. But any child, from the very budding of the intelligence, could grasp the idea of a great, loving Super-Father, who was making Himself visible through gifts and care. If he prayed to Him later he would know to whom he was praying. As it is, the later prayers are neglected, or definitely given up, oftener than not, because this is precisely what the child does not know. He does not know it because he was never taught it; and he was never taught it because his parents have probably not been aware of it themselves.

IV

I myself was never taught it. Notwithstanding all for which I am truly grateful, I regret most deeply that so many years of my life went by before I was led to the fact. I am willing to believe that the lack of understanding was my own fault, but a lack of understanding there was. I got the impression that God, so far from making Himself known to me, was hiding away from me, and that I must have faith to believe in One of whom I had no more than hearsay evidence. If I could do this violence to such measure of reason as I possessed I could count on a reward in some other world than this, though on little or nothing here.

Faith I saw as of the nature of a tour de force. You took it as you took a leap. It was spiritually acrobatic. You didn't understand but you believed. The less you understood the more credit your belief became to you. The more hidden and difficult and mysterious and unintelligible God made Himself the greater your merit in having faith in spite of everything. I am far from saying that this is the common understanding of Christians, or from holding others responsible for my misconceptions. I speak of these misconceptions only because they were mine, and it was I who had to work away from them.

For this reason, too, I speak of my reaching the idea of a God who had been visibly smiling at me all my life while I had never seen Him, as a "discovery." To me it was a discovery; and it came at a moment when I sorely needed something of the kind.

V

It was perhaps three or four years after the turning-point at Versailles. The intervening time had been one of what I may call spiritual ups and downs. It had not all been straight progress by any means. I had got hold of what for me was a great idea, round which other great ideas grouped themselves; but I grasped them waveringly or intermittently. Nevertheless, during seasons in Boston, Nice, Cannes, Munich, London, and Berlin, life on the whole went hopefully. The malady I have already mentioned tended to grow better rather than worse; the advancing blindness became definitely arrested. I worked easily, happily, successfully. Returning to the New England city which had become my adopted home, I bought a house and settled down to American life once more.

I mention these facts only because they help me to make myself clearer. For all at once my affairs, like the chariots of Pharaoh in crossing the Red Sea, began to drive heavily. Trust in an all-conquering life-principle which had meant much to me for a time no longer seemed effective. Difficulties massed themselves. Business misunderstandings sprang up. Friendships on which I had counted suddenly grew cold. Worse than all, the working impulse gave out. There were two whole years in which I slaved at producing little more than what had to be thrown away. My active life had apparently come to another deadening full stop.

I reached the decision that there was but one thing to do—give up the pretence at working, sell the house to which I had grown attached, and resume once more the life of aimless, but at that time inexpensive, European wandering. There came a day when I actually offered my house for sale.

And yet that day proved to be another turning-point. On the very morning when I had put my house in the market the chain of small events which we commonly call accidents brought me into touch with a man I had never seen before. During a first meeting, as well as in several that followed, he made certain matters clear to me which changed my course not only then but ever since. These explanations came under three distinct headings, to each of which I should like to give a little space.

VI

Of these the one I put first is probably familiar to most of my readers, but to me, I confess, it was new.

God among His other functions must be a tireless activity working towards an end. Everything He calls into being works toward that end, I myself with the rest. I am not a purposeless bit of jetsam flung out on the ocean of time to be tossed about helplessly. God couldn't so will an existence. It would not be in keeping with His economy to have any entity wasted. As Our Lord puts it, the sparrow cannot fall without Him; without Him the lilies are not decked; the knowledge possessed by His infinite intelligence is so minute that the very hairs of the head are numbered. My life, my work, myself—all are as much a necessary part of His design as the thread the weaver weaves into the pattern in a carpet.

In other words, I am not a free agent. I am His agent. Not only am I responsible to him, but He is responsible for me. His responsibility for me will be seen as soon as I give up being responsible for myself.

It was upon this last point that I seized with most avidity. I was tired of trying to steer a course for myself, with no compass to go by. I was tired of incessantly travelling along roads which seemed to lead to nothing but blind-ends. To change the figure to one I used not infrequently at that time, my life seemed pitchforked, first in one way and then in another, no way bringing me anywhere. It had no even tenor. It was a series of seismic pulls and jerks.

But in the light of what my new friend told me I saw I had been too busily engaged in directing my life for myself. I was like a child who hopes to make a smoothly working machine go still more smoothly by prodding it. I couldn't leave it alone. It had not occurred to me that the course of that life was God's own business, and that if I could follow the psalmist's advice and "commit my way unto him he would bring it to pass." It had seemed to me that nothing would be brought to pass unless I worried and fretted over it myself, whereas the same wise old psalmist says, in words which our generation would do well to lay to heart, "fret not thyself else shall thou be moved to do evil."

"Trust in the Lord and do good," he goes on; "so shalt thou dwell in the land, and verily thou shalt be fed. Delight thyself also in the Lord, and he shall give thee the desires of thine heart."

This was nothing new; it was only new to me. To feel that I could give up being responsible for results and devote myself to my work was in itself a relief. If I tried to "trust in the Lord and do good"—by which I suppose is meant doing my duty to the best of my small ability—He would look after the rest. My position was somewhat that of a trusted subordinate given a free hand, but having over him a supreme authority taking charge of all consequences. I was not working on what our modern idiom neatly summarises as "my own." I was His agent.

Thus it might be said to be to His interest to see that as His agent I was sheltered, clothed, fed, and in every way kept in such condition as to be up to the highest standard of His work. This provision would naturally include those dependent on me, and without whose well-being I could not have peace of mind. I need worry about them no more than about myself. They, too, were His agents. In certain conditions He might provide for them through me, or in certain conditions He might provide for me through them; but in all conditions He would provide for all of us.

VII

The second point was this: those with whom I had had misunderstandings were equally His agents. They might not be more aware of the fact than I; but this in no way disqualified them as His trusted subordinates given a free hand. Their work with me and mine with them, whatever its nature, wrought one of the infinite number of blends going to make up the vast complexity of His design.

It was, therefore, out of the range of possibility that under Him there could be opposition or contradiction between one of His agents and another. It would be inconsistent with His being that one man's advantage should be brought about at another man's cost. Where that was apparently the case it was due to both sides taking the authority into their own hands, and neither sufficiently recognising Him. If His trusted subordinates in being given a free hand played Him false, they naturally played each other false, and played false to themselves first of all. Where one was afraid of another and strove to outwit him there was treachery against the supreme command.

Again there was nothing new in this; but to me it was a new point of view with regard to those with whom and for whom I worked. For the first time I saw their true relation to me, as mine to them, and something of the principle of brotherhood. Up to this time brotherhood had been a charming, sentimental word to me, and not much more. Children of one Father, yes; but discordant children, with no restraint that I could see on their natural cut-throat enmities.

But here was a truth which made all other men my necessary helpmates, and me the necessary helpmate of all other men. I couldn't do without them; they couldn't do without me. Hostility between us was as out of place as between men pulling together on the rope which is to save all their lives. If peril could bring about unity God could bring it about even more effectively. God was the great positive, the solvent in which irritation and unfriendliness must necessarily melt away.

VIII

The third point, involving my obvious first step, was to put suspicion out of my own mind. I was to see myself as God's Self-Expression working with others who were also His Self-Expression to the same extent as I. It was in the fact of our uniting together to produce His Self-Expression that I was to look for my security. No one could effectively work against me while I was consciously trying to work with God. Moreover, it was probable that no one was working against me, or had any intention of working against me, but that my own point of view being wrong I had put the harmonious action of my life out of order. Suspicion always being likely to see what it suspects the chances were many that I was creating the very thing I suffered from.

This does not mean that in our effort to reproduce harmonious action we should shut our eyes to what is evidently wrong, or blandly ignore what is plainly being done to our disadvantage. Of course not! One uses all the common-sense methods of getting justice for oneself and protecting one's own interests. But it does mean that when I can no longer protect my own interests, when my affairs depend upon others far more than on myself—a condition in which we all occasionally find ourselves—I am not to fret myself, not to churn my spirit into nameless fears. I am not a free agent. Those with whom I am associated are not free agents. God is the one supreme command. He expresses Himself through me; He expresses Himself through them; we all. I as well as they, they as well as I, are partakers of His Sonship; and the Son—His Expression—is always "in the Father's bosom,"[9] in His love and care.

IX

Having grasped this idea the new orientation was not difficult. There was in it too much solace to allow of its being difficult. If I state the results it is once more not because I consider them important to anyone but myself, but only because they became the starting-point of a new advance in the conquest of fear.

Within forty-eight hours, with no action on my part except the Metanoia, the change in my point of view, all misunderstandings had been cleared away. The other side had taken the entire initiative, I making no advance whatever toward them. A telegram expressing their hearty good will was followed by an interview, after which I was at work again. I have not only worked easily ever since but with such fecundity that one plan is always formed before I have its predecessor off my hands. This says nothing of the quality of my work, which, humble as it may be, is simply the best I know how to do. I refer only to its abundance. I have found that in "working together with God," I am less involved in conflicts of wills than I was before, and that the words of Amos are literally fulfilled to me, "that the plowman shall overtake the reaper, and the treader of grapes him that soweth seed." I say it without knocking on wood, and with no fear lest my "good luck" will be withdrawn, that from that time to this I have had plenty of work which I have accomplished happily, and have never lacked a market for my modest wares.

X

From all of which I have drawn one main inference—the imperative urgency of Trust.

I had hitherto thought of trust as a gritting of the teeth and a stiffening of the nerves to believe and endure, no matter what compulsion one put upon oneself. Gradually, in the light of the experience sketched above, I came to see it as simply the knowledge that the supreme command rules everything to everyone's advantage. The more we can rest mentally, keep ourselves at peace, be still and know that it is God,[10] the single and sole Director, the more our interests will be safe. This, I take it, is the kind of trust for which the great pioneers of truth plead so persistently in both the Old and New Testaments.

Trust, then, is not a force we wrest from ourselves against reason, against the grain. To be trust at all it must be loving and spontaneous. It cannot be loving and spontaneous unless there is a natural impulse behind it. And there can be no natural impulse behind it unless we have something in our own experience which corroborates the mere hearsay testimony that there is a Power worth trusting to. Job's "Though He slay me yet will I trust in Him," could only have been wrung from a heart which had proved the Divine Good Will a thousand times and knew what it was doing. Some experience of our own we must have. It is an absolute necessity. Desperate hope in another man's God may do something for us, but it cannot do much. A small thing which I have proved for myself is a better foundation for trust than a Bible learnt parrot-like by rote and not put to the practical test. Once I have found out for myself that to rest in the Lord and wait patiently for Him is the surest way to security and peace I have the more willing confidence in doing it.

God's Self-Expression And The Mind Of To-Day

I

To the mind of to-day trust would be easier were it not for the terror lest God's plans involve us in fearful things from which we shrink. We have heard so much of the trials He sends; of the gifts of Tantalus He keeps forever in our sight but just beyond our reach; of the blessings He actually bestows upon us only to snatch them away when we have come to love them most—we have heard so much of this that we are often afraid of His will as the greatest among the evils of which we stand in dread.

In many cases this is the root of our fear. We cannot trust without misgiving to the love of God. What is there then that we can trust to? We can't trust to ourselves; still less can we trust to our fellow-men. Those whom we love and in whom we have confidence being as weak as ourselves, if not weaker than we, establish our spirits not at all. If, therefore, we mentally poison the well of Universal Good-intent at its very source what have we to depend on?

I have already referred to the God of repressions and denials, and now must speak a little more freely of this travesty on "the Father," as expressed to us in Jesus Christ. Of all the obstacles to the rooting out of fear the lingering belief in such a distortion of Divine Love is to my mind the most deeply based.

I often think it a proof of the vital truth in the message of Jesus Christ that it persists in holding the heart in spite of the ugly thing which, from so many points of view, the Caucasian has managed to make of it. Nowhere is the cruelty of Caucasian misinterpretation more evident than in the meanings given to the glorious phrase, "the Will of God." I do not exaggerate when I say that in most Caucasian minds the Will of God is a bitter, ruthless force, to which we can only drug ourselves into submission. It is always ready to thwart us, to stab us in the back, or to strike us where our affections are tenderest. We hold our blessings only on the tenure of its caprice. Our pleasures are but the stolen moments we can snatch from its inattention.

As an example I quote some stanzas from a hymn frequently sung where English-speaking people worship, and more or less expressive of the whole Caucasian attitude toward "God's Will."

> My God, my Father, while I stray
> Far from my home on life's rough way,
> Oh, teach me from my heart to say,
>   Thy Will be done.

Though dark my path and sad my lot,
Let me be still, and murmur not,
Or breathe the prayer divinely taught,
    Thy Will be done.
What though in lonely grief I sigh
For friends beloved no longer nigh,
Submissive still would I reply,
    Thy Will be done.
If thou shouldst call me to resign
What most I prize, it ne'er was mine;
I only yield thee what is thine;
    Thy Will be done.

These lines, typical of a whole class of sentimental hymnology, are important only in as far as they are widely known and express a more or less standardised point of view. The implication they contain is that all deprivation is brought upon us by the Will of God, and that our wisest course is to beat ourselves down before that which we cannot modify. Beneath the car of this Juggernaut we must flout our judgments and crush our affections. As He knows so well where to hit us we must stifle our moans when He does so. As He knows so well what will ring our hearts we must be content to let Him give so that He can the more poignantly take away. The highest exercise of our own free will is to "be still and murmur not"—to admit that we need the chastisement—to crouch beneath the blows which we tell ourselves are delivered in love, even though it is hard to see where the love comes in.

II

I know nothing more tragic than those efforts on the part of heart-broken people, coming within the experience of all of us, to make themselves feel that this terrible "Will of God" must be right, no matter how much it seems wrong.

A young man with a wife and family to support is struck down by a lingering illness which makes him a burden. All his Job's comforters tell him that God has brought the affliction upon him, and that to bow to the "Inscrutable Will" must be his first act of piety.

A young mother is rejoicing in her baby when its little life is suddenly snuffed out. She must school herself to say, quite irrespective of the spirit of renunciation which inspires the words, "The Lord gave and the Lord hath taken away; blessed be the Name of the Lord."

A woman is left a widow to earn a living for herself, and bring up her children fatherless. She must assume that the Lord had some good purpose in leaving her thus bereft and must drill herself into waiting on a Will so impossible to comprehend.

Storms sink ships, drowning passengers and crew; lightning sets fire to houses and strikes human beings dead; earthquakes swallow up whole districts destroying industry and human life; tidal waves sweep inland carrying away towns; and our legal phraseology can think of no better explanation of such calamity than to ascribe it to "the act of God."

It is needless to multiply these instances. Our own knowledge supplies them by the score. Our personal lives are full of them. God's Will, God's Love, God's Mercy, become strangely ironic forces, grim beyond any open enmity. They remind us of the "love," the "pity," the "mercy," in which the orthodox sent the heretic to the hangman or the stake, destroying the body to save the soul.

It is a far cry from this appalling vision of "the Father" to the psalmist's "Delight thou in the Lord and he shall give thee the desires of thine heart." How could anyone delight in the Caucasian God, as the majority of Caucasians conceive of Him? As a matter of fact, how many Caucasians themselves, however devout, however orthodox, attempt to delight, or pretend to delight, in the God to whom on occasions they bow down? Delight is a strong word, and a lovely one; but used of the Caucasian and his Deity it is not without its elements of humour.

III

Naturally enough! It is impossible for any human being to delight in a God whose first impulse in "doing us good" is so often to ravage our prosperity and affections. So long as we believe in Him fear will rule our lives. It is because the Caucasian believes in Him that he lives in fear and dies in fear. To attempt to eliminate fear and retain this concept of God is vain.

Understanding this the average Caucasian has made little or no effort to eliminate fear. He would rather live and die in fear than change this concept of God. It is dear to him. He finds it useful. To its shoulders he can shift the ills of which he is unwilling himself to accept the responsibility. Where God is a puzzle life is a puzzle; and where life is a puzzle the Caucasian gets his chance for making the materialistic ideal the only one that seems practical. In a world which was to any noticeable degree freed from the spectre of fear most of our existing systems of government, religion, business, law, and national and international politics, would have to be remodelled. There would be little or no use for them. Built on fear and run by fear, fear is as essential to their existence as coal to our industries. A society that had escaped from fear would escape from their control.

In this present spring of 1921 we are having an exhibition of fear on a scale so colossal that the heart of man is dazed by it. There is not a government which is not afraid of some other government. There is not a government which is not afraid of its own people. There is not a people which is not afraid of its own government. There is not a country in which one group is not afraid of some other group. All is rivalry, enmity, suspicion, confusion, and distrust, "while men's hearts are fainting for fear, and for anxious expectation of what is coming on the world." All statesmen, all ministers, all ambassadors, all politicians, all bankers, all business men, all professional men, all journalists, all farmers, all laborers, all workers in the arts, all men and women of all kinds—with the exception of one here and there who has reached the understanding of the love which casteth out fear—live and work in fear, and in mistrust of their colleagues. From the supreme councils of the Allies down to the crooks and conspirators in dives and joints everyone is afraid of being double-crossed. There is so much double-crossing everywhere that we have been obliged to invent this name for the operation. England is afraid of being double-crossed by Germany, France by England, Italy by France, the United States by Europe, and Japan by the United States, while within these general limitations minor double-crossing interests seethe like bacteria in a drop of poisoned blood. The nations are infected with fear because they elect to believe in a God of fear, and the Caucasians more than others because they have chosen to see a God of fear in Him who was put before them as a God of Love.

IV

I see no way out of all this except as one of us after another reaches the Metanoia, the new point of view as regards God. Other ways have been sought, and have been found no more than blind alleys. Much reference is made nowadays to the disillusionment of those who hoped that the war would lead to social and spiritual renovation; but any such hope was doomed in advance, so long as the Caucasian concept of God was unchanged. When you cannot trust God you cannot trust anything; and when you cannot trust anything you get the condition of the world as it is to-day. And that you cannot trust a God whose "love" will paralyse the hand by which you have to earn a living, or snatch your baby from your breast—to say nothing of a thousand ingenious forms of torture inflicted just because "He sees that it is best for you," after having led you to see otherwise—that you cannot trust a God like that must be more or less self-evident. If you are part of His Self-Expression He cannot practise futilities through your experience and personality. He must be kind with a common-sense kindness, loving with a common-sense love. Whatever explanation of our sufferings and failures there may be we must not shuffle them off on God. "Let us hold God to be true," St. Paul writes, "though every man should prove false."[11] Let us hold that God would not hurt us, however much we may wilfully hurt each other or ourselves.

V

I should not lay so much emphasis on this if so much emphasis were not laid on it in the other direction. God has so persistently, and for so many generations, been held up to us as a God who tries and torments and punishes that we can hardly see Him as anything else. Torture comes, in the minds of many of us, to be not only His main function but His only function. "I am all right," is the unspoken thought in many a heart, "so long as I am not overtaken by the Will of God. When that calamity falls on me my poor little human happiness will be wrecked like a skiff in a cyclone." This is not an exaggeration. It is the secret mental attitude of perhaps ninety percent of those Caucasians who believe in a God of any kind. Their root-conviction is that if God would only let them alone they would get along well enough; but as a terrible avenging spirit, like the Fury or the Nemesis of the ancients, he is always tracking them down. The aversion from God so noticeable in the mind of to-day is, I venture to think, chiefly inspired by the instinct to get away from, or to hide from, the pursuit of this Avenger.

VI

And in a measure this impulse to flight can be understood. I can understand that common-sense men should be cold toward the Caucasian God, and that they should even renounce and denounce him. I will go so far as to say that I can more easily understand the atheist than I can many of my own friends who pathetically try to love and adore their capricious un-Christlike Deity. To my certain knowledge many of them are doing it against their own natural and better instincts, because they dare not forsake the tradition in which they have been dyed. "I try to love God and I can't," has been said to me many a time by conscientious people who felt that the fault must lie in themselves. There was no fault in themselves. If their God could have been loved they would have loved him.

VII

I come here to a point of no small importance to the conquest of fear, the courage to release oneself from the tether of tradition. Few people have it, in the sense of rejecting old theories because of having worked out to new spiritual knowledge. When it comes to the eternal verities many of us are cowardly; nearly all of us are timid. The immense majority of us prefer a God at second or third hand. We will accept what somebody else has learned, rather than incur the trouble or the responsibility of learning anything for ourselves. We take our knowledge of God as we take our doses of medicine, from a prescription which one man has written down, and another has "put up," and still another administers. By the time this traditional, handed-on knowledge of God has reached ourselves it is diluted by all kinds of outside opinions and personalities. It is not strange that when we have swallowed the dose it does little to effect a cure. I do not deny that a second or third hand knowledge of God may do something. I only deny that it can do much. To support my denial I need only point to what the world has become in a second and third hand Christendom. The illustration is enough.

It should be plain, I think, that no one will ever be released from fear by clinging to the teachings which have inspired fear. We are fearless in proportion as we grow independent enough to know for ourselves. I cannot but stress this point to some extent, for the reason that I myself suffered so long from inability to let the traditional go. It seemed to me to have a sanctity just because it was traditional. The fact that other people had accepted certain ideas had weight in making me feel that I should accept them too. To go off on a line of my own seemed dangerous. I might make mistakes. I might go far wrong. Safety was spelled by hanging with the crowd.

It was the chance remark of an old acquaintance which dislodged me from this position. In the lobby of a hotel we had met by chance, after not having seen each other for a good many years. The conversation, having touched on one theme and another, drifted to subjects akin to that which I am now discussing. I ventured to disclose some of my own "seeking God, if perhaps I could grope for Him and find Him."[12]

My friend straightened himself and squared his shoulders. "I stand exactly where I did thirty years ago."

There was a pride in the statement with regard to which my first feeling was a pang of envy. A rapid calculation told me that thirty years ago he had been about twenty; and the superiority of a man who at twenty had attained to so much spiritual insight that he had not needed to learn anything more in the interim was evident. I was two or three days turning this incident over in my mind before the exclamation came to me, "How terrible!" To have lived through the thirty years of the richest experience the ordinary man ever knows and still have remained on precisely the same spot as to spiritual things struck me then as a woeful confession.

I beg to say here that I am not talking of external and official religious connections. I am trying to avoid the subject of external and official religion altogether. I am speaking not of religion but of God. To my mind the two have no more than the relation of the words of a song and the music of its setting. You may use them together or you may consider them apart. I am considering them apart, and confining myself wholly to the words of the song. What is known as church-affiliation, the music of the setting, I am not concerned with. My only topic is the way in which the meaning of the words gets over to the average inner man, and the effect upon him mentally.

I revert, therefore, to the statement that to make the kind of spiritual progress which will overcome fear it will be often necessary to let go the thing we have outlived. Often the thing we have outlived will be something dear to us, because there was once a time when it served our turn. But our turn to-day may need something different from the turn of yesterday, and the refusal to follow new light simply because it is new leads in the end to mental paralysis. I was once asked to sign a petition to the mayor of a city praying that, on the ground of its novelty, electric lighting might be excluded from the street in which I lived. Exactly this same reluctance often keeps us from making changes of another sort, even when we feel that the light which hitherto was enough for us has been outgrown and outclassed.

The danger of the lone quest leading a man astray can be easily exaggerated. It is not as if God were difficult to find. "The soul cannot move, wake, or open the eyes, without perceiving God." "For this commandment which I command thee this day, it is not hidden from thee, neither is it far off. It is not in heaven that thou shouldest say, Who shall go up for us to heaven and bring it down unto us that we may hear it and do it? Neither is it beyond the sea that thou shouldest say, Who shall go over the sea for us and bring it unto us that we may hear it and do it? But the word is very nigh unto thee, in thy mouth and in thy heart."[13] No motion toward the Universal can miss the Universal. I cannot escape from the Ever-Present; the Ever-Present cannot escape from me. Intellectually I may make mistakes in deduction, but spiritually I cannot but find God. The little I learn of God for myself is to me worth more than all the second and third hand knowledge I can gather from the saints.

VIII

It is the more necessary to dwell on this for the reason that whatever Metanoia, or new orientation, is to be brought about must be on the part of individuals. There is no hope for large numbers acting together, or for any kind of group-impulse. Group-impulse among Caucasians is nearly always frightened, conservative, reactionary, or derisive of the forward step. There is hardly an exception to this in the whole history of Caucasian ideas.

Otherwise it would be a pleasant dream to imagine what might now be happening on the great international stage. Let us suppose that the leaders of the so-called Christian countries were all convinced of the three main lines of God's direction I have already tried to sketch. Let us think of such men as Lloyd George, Clemenceau, Sforza, President Harding, and the heads of government in Belgium, Russia, Germany, and all other countries affected by the present war of moves and counter-moves—let us think of them as agreed on the principles:

1. That each knows himself and his country as an agent in the hand of God, directed surely toward a good end;

2. That each knows each of his colleagues and his country as equally an agent in the hand of God, directed surely toward a similar good end;

3. That each knows that between God's agents there can be neither conflicting interests nor clash of wills, and that suspicion and counter-suspicion must be out of place, since under God's direction no double-crossing is possible.

The picture is almost comic in its incongruity with what actually is. The mere thought of these protagonists of the century working in harmony to one great purpose, without distrust of each other's motives, and with no necessity for anyone's dodging political foul play, summons the smile of irony. Mutual trust was never so much a suggestion to laugh down. The mere hint that it might be possible would make one a target for the wit of the experienced.

In what we call the practical world of to-day there is no appeal from the God of Fear but to the God of Fear. The great mass of Caucasians will not have it otherwise. And it requires no prophetic vision to foresee the results of the efforts to bring about international harmony while all are obeying the decrees of the Goddess of Discord. Nearly three years after the signing of the armistice the world is in a more hopeless situation than it was when at war. Up to the present each new move only makes matters worse. There are those who believe that our phase of civilisation is staggering into the abyss and that nothing, as far as can now be descried, will save it from the deluge.

IX

Possibly! Fear tends always to produce the thing it is afraid of. I mention this dark outlook only for the reason that even if the cataclysm were to come the individual can escape from it.

Cataclysms are not new in the history of our race. The rise and fall of civilisations may be called mankind's lessons in "how not to do it." Of these lessons there are no such records as those which we find in the Old Testament;

and in these records it is unfailingly pointed out that whatever the calamity which overtakes the world at large the individual has, if he chooses, a way of safety. The innocent are not overwhelmed with the guilty, except when the innocent deliberately shut their eyes to the opening toward the Soteria—the Safe Return. But that, unhappily, the innocent do so shut their eyes is one of the commonest facts in life.

Back in that twilight of history of which the later tale could be told only by some symbol, some legendary hieroglyph, there was already an "Ark" by which the faithful few could be saved from the "Flood." The symbol became permanent. The Ark of the Covenant—the sign of a great spiritual understanding—remained as a token to man that in God he had a sure refuge. It was laid up in his Holy of Holies, a mystic, consecrated pledge, till the ruthless Caucasian came and rifled it.

But no rifling could deprive mankind of its significance. That endures. To bring it home to the desolate and oppressed was a large part of the mission of psalmists and prophets. The Ark of the Covenant—of the Great Understanding—meant as much to those who sought God in the ancient world as the Cross does to Christendom. It meant that whatever the collapse, national or general, through siege or sack or famine, those who would escape could escape by the simple process of mentally taking refuge in God. The Ark of God would bear them safely when all material help failed.

Among the themes which run through the Old Testament this is of paramount importance. It is impossible to do more than refer to the many times the spiritually minded were implored to seek this protection. It was needful to implore them since they found the assurance so difficult to believe. No matter how often it was proved to them they still doubted it. Saved by this method once they would reject it when it came to danger the second time. Saved the second time they rejected it the third. "Thou shalt keep him in perfect peace whose mind is stayed on thee, because he trusteth in thee," is the declaration of Jeremiah, who perhaps more than any other was a prophet of disaster. Similar statements are scattered through the Old Testament by the score, by the hundred. It was a point on which leaders, seers, and teachers insisted with a passionate insistence. They knew. They had tested the truth for themselves. Disaster was a common feature in their history. During the three thousand years and more which their experiences cover these Israelites had seen more than one invasion sweep across their land, more than one civilisation come and go. All that Belgium knew in the Great War they knew time and time again. Between Egypt and Assyria, the France and Germany of that special epoch, theirs was a kind of buffer state over which every new anguish rolled. "Let it roll," was the cry of their prophets. "The Lord will fight for you. Stand still and see what he will do. His arm is not shortened neither his strength diminished. It is of the Lord to save whether by many or by few. Trust in the Lord and be doing good, so shalt thou dwell in the land, and verily thou shalt be fed. Oh, how great is thy goodness which thou hast wrought for them that trust in thee before the sons of men. I said in my haste, I am cut off! Nevertheless thou heardest the voice of my supplication when I cried unto thee. Be of good courage and he shall strengthen your heart, all ye that hope in the Lord."[14]

X

In many ways this is the burden of the more ancient Scriptures—the protection which surrounds those who know that protection is God. It was a gospel that had to be preached with tears and beseechings from one generation to another. No generation accepted it. The belief in material power was always too dense. It is still too dense. In the Ark of the Great Understanding the Caucasian has practically never seen more than a symbol that has gone out of date. Lost materially in the Tiber mud it was, for him, lost forever. But not so. Its significance remains as vital to mankind as when, veiled and venerated, it stood between the cherubim.

The time may be close at hand when we shall need this assurance as we need nothing else. However optimistic we try to keep ourselves, no thinking man or woman can be free, at this crisis in world-history, from deep foreboding. For the memory to go back ten years is, even for us in the New World, like returning to a Golden Age; while for the Old World mere recollection must be poignant.

The possibility that all countries in both hemispheres may find themselves in some such agony as that of the Russia of to-day is not too extravagant to be entertained. This is not saying that they are likely so to find themselves; it means only that in the world as it is the safest is not very safe. My point is that whether catastrophe overwhelms us or not, he who chooses not to fear can be free from fear. There is a refuge for him, a defence, a safeguard which no material attack can break down. "He that dwelleth in the secret place of the Most High shall abide under the shadow of the Almighty. I will say of the Lord, He is my refuge—my fortress—my God. In Him will I trust."[15] There is this Ark for me, this Ark of the Great Understanding, and I can retire into it. I can also have this further assurance: "Because thou hast made the Lord which is my refuge—even the Most High—thy habitation, there shall no evil befall thee, neither shall any plague come nigh thy dwelling. For he shall give his angels charge over thee to keep thee in all thy ways."[16]

XI

This is the eternal agreement, but an agreement of which we find it difficult to accept the terms. To the material alone we are in the habit of ascribing power. Though we repeat a thousand times in the course of a year, "For thine is the kingdom, the power, and the glory," we do not believe it. To few of us is it more than a sonorous phrase.

I remember the impression of this which one received at the great thanksgiving for peace in St. Paul's Cathedral in London some twenty years ago. The Boer War had ended in an English victory, and while the thanksgiving was not precisely for this, it did express the relief of an anxious nation that peace was again restored. It was what is generally known as a most impressive service. All that a great spectacle can offer to God it offered. King, queen, princes, princesses, ambassadors, ministers, clergy, admirals, generals, and a vast assembly of citizens filled the choir and nave with colour and life, while the music was of that passionless beauty of which the English cathedral choirs guard the secret.

But the detail I remember best was the way in which the repetition of the Lord's Prayer rolled from the lips of the assembly like the sound of the surging of the sea. It was the emotional effect of a strongly emotional moment. One felt tense. It was hard to restrain tears. As far as crowd-sympathy has any spiritual value it was there. The Caucasian God was taken out of His pigeon-hole and publicly recognised.

Then He was put back.

I take this service merely as an instance of what happens in all the so-called Christian capitals in moments of national stress. Outwardly it happens less in the United States than it does elsewhere, for the reason that this country has no one representative spiritual expression; but it does happen here in diffused and general effect. As a Christian nation we ascribe in common with other Christian nations the kingdom, the power, and the glory to God—on occasions. We do it with the pious gesture and the sonorous phrase. Then we forget it. The habit of material trust is too strong for us. Kings, queens, presidents, princes, prime ministers, congresses, parliaments, and all other representatives of material strength, may repeat for formal use the conventional clause; but there is always what we flippantly know as a "joker" in the lip-recitation. "Kingdom, power, and glory," we can hear ourselves saying in a heart-aside, "lie in money, guns, commerce, and police. God is not sufficiently a force in the affairs of this world for us to give Him more than the consideration of an act of courtesy."

Practically that is all we ever get from group-impulse—an act of courtesy. I repeat and repeat again that whatever is done toward the conquest of fear must be done by the individual. I must do what I can to conquer fear in myself, regardless of the attitude or opinions of men in general.

To men in general the appeal to spiritual force to bring to naught material force is little short of fanatical. It has never been otherwise as yet; it will probably not be otherwise for long generations to come. Meanwhile it is much for the individual to know that he can act on his own initiative, and that when it comes to making God his refuge he can go into that refuge alone. He needs no nation, or government, or society, or companions before him or behind him. He needs neither leader nor guide nor friend. In the fortress of God he is free to enter merely as himself, and there know that he is safe amid a world in agony.

XII

This is not theory; it is not doctrine; it is not opinion. It is what the great pioneers of truth have first deduced from what they understood to be the essential beneficence of God, and then proved by actual demonstration. Anyone else can demonstrate it who chooses to make the experiment. My own weakness is such that I have made the experiment but partially; but partial experiment convinces me beyond all further questioning that the witness of the great pioneers is true.

XIII

Nor is this conviction to be classed as idealism, or ecclesiasticism, or mysticism, or anything else to which we can put a tag. It is not sectarian; it is not peculiarly Christian. It is the general possession of mankind. True, it is easier for the Christian than for any other to enter on this heritage, since his spiritual descent is more directly from the pioneers of truth who first discovered God to be His children's safety; but the Universal is the Universal, the property of all. Discovery gives no one an exclusive hold on it. Anyone with a consciousness of Almighty, Ever-Present Intelligence must have some degree of access to it, though his access may not be to the fullest or the easiest. It is not possible that the Universal Father should be the special property of the Christian or of anyone else. The Christian view of the Father is undoubtedly the truest; but every view is true in proportion to its grasp of truth. No one will deny that the Buddhist, the Mahometan, the Confucianist, have their grasp of truth. Even the primitive idolater has some faint gleam of it, distorted though it may have become. Very well, then; the faintest gleam of such knowledge will not go without its recompense.

XIV

Exclusiveness is too much our Caucasian habit of mind. It is linked with our instinct for ownership. Because through Jesus Christ we have a clearer view of a greater segment of the Universal, if I may so express myself, than the Buddhist can have through Buddha or the Mahometan through Mahomet, our tendency is to think that we know the whole of the Universal, and have it to give away. Any other view of the Universal is to us so false as to merit not merely condemnation but extirpation. Extirpation has been the watchword with which Caucasian Christianity has gone about the world. We have taken toward other views of truth no such sympathetic stand as St. Paul to that which he found in Greece, and which is worth recalling:

"Men of Athens, I perceive that you are in every respect remarkably religious. For as I passed along and observed the things you worship, I found also an altar with this inscription, TO THE UNKNOWN GOD. The Being, therefore, whom you, without knowing it, revere, Him I now proclaim to you. God who made the universe and everything in it—He being Lord of heaven and earth—does not dwell in sanctuaries built by men. Nor is He administered to by human hands as though He needed anything—but He Himself gives to all men life and breath and all things. He caused to spring from one forefather people of every race, for them to live on the whole surface of the earth, and marked for them an appointed span of life, and the boundaries of their homes; that they might seek God, if perhaps they might grope for Him and find Him. Yes, though He is not far from any one of us. For it is in closest union with Him that we live and move and have our being; as in fact some of the poets in repute among yourselves have said, 'For we are also His offspring.'"[17]

To the conquest of fear this splendid universalism is another essential. God being "not far from any one of us" cannot be far from me. He who gives to all men life and breath and all things will not possibly deny me the things I require most urgently. Our whole civilisation may go to pieces; the job by which I earn a living may cease to be a job; the money I have invested may become of no more value than Russian bonds; the children whom I hoped I had provided for may have to face life empty-handed; all my accustomed landmarks may be removed, and my social moorings swept away; nevertheless, the Universal cannot fail me. "Although the figtree shall not blossom nor fruit be in the vines; though the labour of the olive shall fail, and the fields yield no meat; though the flocks be cut off from the fold and there be no herd in the stalls; yet I will rejoice in God, I will joy in the God of my salvation." It is safe to say that this confidence on the part of Habakkuk was not due to mere grim forcing of the will. It was the fruit of experience, of knowledge, of demonstration. In spite of the dangers national and personal he saw threatening, his certainty of God must have been spontaneous.

Anyone, in any country, in any epoch, and of any creed or no creed, who has shared this experience shares also this assurance. To the Christian it comes easiest; but that it does not come easy even to the Christian is a matter of common observation. It can only come easily when some demonstration has been made for oneself, after which there is no more disputing it.

XV

Nor is it a question of morals or morality.

I must venture here on delicate ground and say what I should hesitate to say were the contrary not so strongly underscored. I mean that God, from what we understand to be His nature, could not accord us His protection by weighing the good and the evil in our conduct, and giving or withholding help according to our worthiness. The Universal is too great to be measured and doled in that way. Nothing but our own pinchbeck ideas could ascribe to Him this pettiness. As it is the kind of sliding scale we ourselves adopt, we limit the Divine Generosity by our own limitations.

Not so was the understanding of Jesus Christ. That we should be kind to the so-called evil as we are to the so-called good was a point on which He dwelt in the Sermon on the Mount. To discriminate between them when it comes to the possibility of conferring benefits is in His opinion small. "You have heard that it was said, 'Thou shalt love thy neighbor, and hate thine enemy.' But I command you all, Love your enemies, and pray for your persecutors; that so you may become true sons of your Father in heaven. For He causes His sun to rise on the wicked as well as on the good, and sends rain upon those who do right and those who do wrong."[18]

In other words, we are not to feel ourselves turned out of our "habitation" in God by a sense of our moral lapses. Moral lapses are to be regretted, of course; but they do not vitiate our status as the Sons of God. It is possible that no one believes they do; but much of the loose statement current among those who lay emphasis on morals would give that impression. There is a whole vernacular in vogue in which souls are "lost" or "saved" according to the degree to which they conform or do not conform to other people's views as to what they ought to do. Much of our pietism is to the effect that God is at the bestowal not merely of a sect, but of some section of a sect, and cannot be found through any other source.

XVI

This brings me to the distinction between morals and righteousness, which is one for the mind of to-day to keep as clearly as possible before it. I have said that the refuge in God is not a question of morals; but it is one of righteousness. Between righteousness and morals the difference is important.

Morals stand for a code of observances; righteousness for a direction of the life.

Morals represent just what the word implies, the customs of an age, a country, or a phase in civilisation. They have no absolute standard. The morals of one century are not those of another. The morals of one race are not those of another even in the same century. In many respects the morals of the Oriental differ radically from those of the Occidental, age-long usage being behind each. It is as hard to convince either that his are the inferior as it would be to make him think so of his mother-tongue. I once asked a cultivated Chinaman, a graduate of one of the great American universities and a Christian of the third generation, in what main respect he thought China superior to the United States. "In morals," he replied, promptly; but even as a Christian educated in America his theory of morals was different from ours.

Among ourselves in the United States the essence of morals is by no means a subject of unanimous agreement. You might say that a standard of morals is entirely a matter of opinion. There are millions of people who think it immoral to play cards, to go to the theatre, to dance, or to drink wine. There are millions of other people who hold all these acts to be consistent with the highest moral conduct.

Moreover, wherever the emphasis is thrown on morals as distinct from righteousness there is a tendency to put the weight on two or three points in which nations or individuals excel, and to ignore the rest. For example, not to go outside ourselves, the American people may be fairly said to exemplify two of the great virtues: On the whole they are, first, sober; secondly, continent. As a result we accentuate morals in these respects, but not in any others.

For instance, the current expression, "an immoral man," is almost certain to apply only under the two headings cited above, and probably only under one. All other morals and immoralities go by the board. We should not class a dishonest man as an immoral man, nor an untruthful man, nor a profane, or spiteful, or ungenial, or bad-tempered, man. Our notion of morals hardly ever rises above the average custom of the community in which we happen to live. Except in the rarest instances we never pause to reflect as to whether the customs of that community are or are not well founded. The consequence is that our cities, villages, countrysides, and social groupings are filled with men and women moral enough as far as the custom of the country goes, but quite noticeably unrighteous.

It is also a fact that where you find one or two virtues singled out for observance and the rest obscured there you find, too, throngs of outwardly "moral" people with corroded hearts. Villages, churches, and all the quieter communities are notorious for this, the peculiarity having formed for a hundred and fifty years the stock-in-trade of novelists. Sobriety and continence being more or less in evidence the assumption is that all the requirements have been fulfilled. The community is "moral" notwithstanding the back-bitings, heart-burnings, slanders, cheatings, envies, hatreds, and bitternesses that may permeate it through and through. As I write, the cramped, venomous, unlovely life of the American small town is the favourite theme of our authors and readers of fiction. Since a number of the works now on the market have met with national approval one must assume that the pictures they paint are accurate. The conditions are appalling, but, according to the custom of the country, they are "moral." The shadow of insobriety and incontinence doesn't touch the characters who move across these pages, and yet the level of the life is pictured as debased, and habits as hideous.

XVII

With morals in this accepted American sense righteousness has little to do. The two are different in origin. Morals imply the compulsion of men, and are never more binding than the customs of men render them. They are thus imposed from without, while righteousness springs from within. The essence of righteousness lies in the turning of the individual toward God.

I think it safe to say that righteousness is expressed more accurately in attitude than in conduct. It is expressed in conduct, of course; but conduct may fail while the attitude can remain constant. It is worthy of remark that some of the great examples of righteousness cited in the Bible were conspicuously sinners. That is to say, they were men of strong human impulses against which they were not always sufficiently on guard, but who turned towards God in spite of everything. In the long line spanning the centuries between Noah and Abraham and Peter and Paul—from the almost prehistoric out into the light of day—not one is put before us except in his weakness as well as in his strength. Some of them commit gross sins; but apparently even gross sins do not debar them from their privileges in God's love. This principle was expressed in the words of Samuel: "Fear not: ye have done all this wickedness; yet turn not aside from following the Lord.... For the Lord will not forsake his people for his great name's sake." That the Universal who has all the blessings of creation to bestow should deprive me of anything just because in my folly or weakness I have committed sins is not consistent with "his great name's sake." It would not be causing His sun to rise on the wicked as well as on the good nor sending rain on those who do right and those who do wrong. I am too small for His immensity to crush with its punishments, but not too small to be the object of His entire love.

XVIII

I hope it is plain that I say this not to make little of doing wrong but to put the love and fulness of God in the dominating place. I must make it clear to myself that He does not shut me out of His heart because I am guilty of sins. I may shut myself out of His heart, unless I direct my mind rightly; but He is always there, unchanged, unchangeable, the ever-loving, ever-welcoming Father. Whatever I have done I can return to Him with the knowledge that He will take me back. Far from sure of myself, I can always be sure of Him.

There are those who would warn me against saying this through fear lest it should be interpreted as, "Don't be afraid to sin so long as you keep mentally close to God." I prefer to run that risk. The dread figure of "an angry God" has been so worked to terrorise men that large numbers of us have been terrorised. But experience shows us every day that being terrorised never produces the results at which it aims. It does not win us; it drives us away.

Much of the alienation from God in the mind of to-day is due to rebellion on the part of our sense of justice. We are sinners, of course; but not such sinners as to merit the revenge which an outraged deity is described as planning against us. That the All-loving and All-mighty should smite us in our dearest aims or our sweetest affections just because we have not conformed to the lop-sided morality of men is revolting to our instincts. We are repulsed by the God of Fear when we are drawn, comforted, strengthened, and changed by Him who is never anything toward us but "the Father."

I have no hesitation, therefore, in throwing the emphasis in what I have to say on the fact that He is "a place to hide me in"—the Ark of the Great Understanding—always open to my approach—into which, whatever I have done, I can go boldly.

The Mind Of To-Day And The World As It Is

I

Much of what I have written will seem inconsistent with the fact that in the world as it is there are undeniable and inevitable hardships. True! I do not escape them more than any other man, the relative relief from fear saving me from only some of them.

I have not meant to say that even with one's refuge in God there is nothing left to struggle with. My point is that whatever there may be to struggle with there is nothing to be afraid of. Freedom from struggle would profit us not at all. On the contrary, it would render us nerveless, flabby, flaccid, and inert.

But fear, as a rule, being connected with our struggles, it is important, I think, to be as clear as we can concerning the purport of those struggles, and their source. We have already seen that fear is diminished in proportion as we understand that our trials are not motiveless, and perhaps this is the point at which to consider briefly what the motives are.

II

Struggle we may define as the act of wrestling with trial, so as to come out of it victoriously. It is a constant element in every human life. Furthermore, I am inclined to think that, taking trial as an average, the amount which enters into one life differs little from that which enters into another.

There was a time when I did not think so. Some lives struck me as singled out for trouble; others were left comparatively immune from it. One would have said that destinies had been mapped with a strange disregard for justice. Those who didn't deserve it suffered; those whom suffering might have purified went scot free. Some were rich, others were poor; some had high positions, others humble ones; some had the respect of the world from the day they were born, others crept along from birth to death in restriction and obscurity. The contrasts were so cruel that they scorched the eyes of the soul.

This is true, of course; and I am not saying that in the testing to which everyone is subjected all have an equal share of the opportunities for triumphing. I am speaking for the moment only of the degree to which the testing comes. As to that, I am inclined to feel that there is little to choose between one life and another, since each of us seems to be tried for all that he can bear.

One is impressed with that in one's reading of biography. Only the lives of what we may call the favoured few get into print, and of those few it is chiefly the external events that are given us. Glimpses of the inner experience may be obtained from time to time, but they are rarely more than glimpses. Of what the man or the woman has endured in the secret fastnesses of the inner life practically nothing can be told. And yet even with the little that finds its way into words how much there is of desperate fighting. To this there is never an exception. The great statesman, the great poet, the great priest, the great scientist, the great explorer, the great painter, the great novelist—not one but suffers as anyone suffers, and of not one would the reader, as a rule, put himself in the place.

I bring up this fact because we so often feel that the other man has an easier task than ourselves. The very thing I lack is that with which he is blessed. I see him smiling and debonair at the minute when I am in a ferment. While I hardly know how to make both ends meet he is building a big house or buying a new motor-car. While I am burying hope or love he is in the full enjoyment of all that makes for happiness and prosperity.

We are always prone to contrast our darker minutes with our friends' brighter ones. We forget, or perhaps we never know, that they do the same with us. At times we are as much the object of their envy as they ever are of ours.

I say this not on the principle that misery loves company, but in order to do away with the heathen suspicion lingering in many minds that God singles me out for trial, heaping benefits on others who deserve them no more than I do.

God singles no one out for trial. When trials come they spring, as nearly as I can observe, from one or all of the three following sources. There are:

A. The trials which come from a world of matter;

B. The trials which come from a world of men;

C. The trials we bring on ourselves.

III

A. The minute we speak of matter we speak of a medium which the mind of to-day is just beginning to understand. The mind of other days did not understand it at all. Few phases of modern advance seem to me more significant of a closer approach to the understanding of spiritual things than that which has been made along these lines.

To all the generations before our own matter was a sheer and positive density. Its hardness, solidity, and actuality could not be gainsaid. Earth was earth; iron was iron; wood was wood. Blood was blood; flesh was flesh; bone was bone. A man was a material being attached to a material planet, as a sponge is attached to the bottom of the sea. All that he touched and ate and wore and used was of the same material Absolute. As to the spiritual there could be a question; as to the material there could be none. The speculation of occasional philosophers, that matter might not after all be more than a mental phenomenon, was invariably hooted down. "I know that matter is matter by standing on it," are in substance the words attributed to even so spiritually-minded a man as the great Dr. Johnson. On this point, as perhaps on some others, he may be taken as a spokesman for the Caucasian portion of our race.

And now comes modern physical science reducing matter to a tenuousness only one remove from the purely spiritual, if it is as much as that. Gone is the mass of the mountains, the stoniness of rocks, the hard solidity of iron. The human body, as someone puts it, is no more than a few pails of water and a handful of ash. Ash and water are alike dissipated into gases, and gases into elements more subtle still. Keeping strictly to the material modern science has reached the confines of materiality. Where it will lead us next no man knows.

But the inference is not unfair that the world of matter is to a considerable degree, and perhaps altogether, a world of man's own creation. That is to say, while God is doing one thing with it, the human mind understands another. For the human point of view to develop and develop and develop till it becomes identical with God's is perhaps the whole purpose of existence.

IV

To me personally it was no small help in overcoming fear when I saw the purpose of existence as expressed in the single word, Growth. That, at least, is a legitimate inference to draw from the history of life on this planet. Assuming that the universe contains an intelligible design of any sort, and that life on this planet is part of it, a vast development going on eternally toward complete understanding of Infinite Right and Happiness would give us some explanation of the mystery of our being here. Beginning, for reasons at which we can only guess, far away from that understanding, we are forever approaching it, with forever the joy of something new to master or to learn. New perceptions, new comprehensions, new insights gained, new victories, even little victories, won, constitute, I think, our treasures laid up in that heaven where neither moth nor wear-and-tear destroys, and where thieves do not break in and steal. Where this treasure is, there, naturally enough, our hearts will be also. Looking back over the ages since the life-principle first glided into our planet waters—how it did so is as yet part of our unsolved mystery—what we chiefly see is a great surging of the living thing upward and upward toward that Highest Universal to which we give the name of God.

V

That is a point which we do not sufficiently seize—that God is not revealed to us by one avenue of truth alone, but by all the avenues of truth working together. With our tendency to keep the Universal in a special compartment of life we see Him as making Himself known through a line of teachers culminating in a Church or a complex of churches; and we rarely think of Him as making Himself known in any other way. To change the figure, He trickles to us like a brook instead of bathing us round and round like light or air.

But all good things must express the Universal; and all discovery of truth, whether by religion, science, philosophy, or imaginative art, must be discovery in God. The Ten Commandments and the Sermon on the Mount are discoveries in God, but so are the advances in knowledge made by Plato, Aristotle, Roger Bacon, and Thomas Edison. He shows Himself through Abraham, Moses, Isaiah, and St. Paul, but also through Homer, Shakespeare, Michael Angelo, Beethoven, Darwin, George Eliot, William James, and Henry Irving. I take the names at random as illustrating different branches of endeavour, and if I use only great ones it is not that the lesser are excluded. No one department of human effort is specially His, or is His special expression. The Church cannot be so more than the stage, or music more than philosophy. His Holy Spirit can be no more outpoured on the bishop or the elder for his work than on the inventor or the scientist for his work. I say so not to minimise the outpouring on the bishop or the elder, but to magnify that on everyone working for progress. This, I take it, is what St. John means when he says, "God does not give the Spirit with limitations." He who always gives all to all His children cannot give more.

When our Lord restores sight to a blind man, or Peter and John cause a lame man to walk, we see manifestations of God; but we see equal manifestations of God when one man gives us the telephone, another the motor-car, and another wireless telegraphy. Whatever declares His power declares Him; and whatever declares Him is a means by which we press upward to the perception of His loving almightiness. The advance may be irregular but it is advance; and all advance is advance toward Him.

VI

That is to say, we are rising above a conception of life in which matter is our master; and yet we are rising above it slowly. This is my chief point here, because by understanding it we see why we still suffer from material afflictions. We have overcome some of them, but only some of them. It is a question of racial development. As we glance backward we see how much of the way we have covered; as we look round on our present conditions we see how much there is still to be achieved.

To diminish fear we should have it, I think, clearly before us that the human race has done as yet only part of its work, and put us in possession of only part of the resources which will one day belong to us. If we could compare ourselves with our ancestors in the days, let us say, of Christopher Columbus or William the Conqueror we should seem in relation to them like children of a higher phase of creation. If we could compare ourselves with our descendants of five hundred or a thousand years hence we should probably be amazed at our present futility and grossness. Our ancestors in the Middle Ages could do certain great things, as we, too, can do certain great things; but in general access to the Universal Storehouse which is God we have made progress in ways unknown to them, as our children will make such progress after us.

But we have made only the progress we have made. We have its advantages, but there are advantages to which we have not yet attained. We might liken ourselves to people who have reached the fourth or fifth step of a stairway in which there are twenty or thirty. We have climbed to a certain height, but we are far from having reached the plane to which we are ascending.

VII

It is worth noting this for the reason that we are so likely to think of ourselves as the climax to which the ages have worked up, and after which there is no beyond. We are the final word, or as the French express it, the last cry, le dernier cri. All that can be felt we have felt, all that can be known we have experienced. For the most part this stand is taken by the intellectuals in all modern countries. In us of to-day, of this very hour, the wave of Eternity has broken, throwing nothing at our feet but froth. The literature of the past ten years is soaked in the pessimism of those who regret that this should be all that the travail of Time could produce for us.

In view of this moan from so many of the writers who have the public ear, especially in Europe, it is the more important to keep before us the fact that we are children of a race but partially developed at best. Compared with what will one day be within human scope our actual reach is only a little beyond impotence. I say this not merely at a venture, but on the strength of what has happened in the past. We are not a people which has accomplished much, but one on the way to accomplishment. The achievements of which we can boast are relatively like those of a child of five who boasts that he can count. Our whole world-condition shows us to be racially incompetent, and able to produce no more than incompetent leaders. That is our present high-water mark, and with our high-water mark we must learn to be satisfied.

Escaping from matter we are still within the grasp of matter, and shall probably so continue for generations to come. Our struggles must therefore be largely with matter, till little by little we achieve its domination. In proportion as the individual does so now he reaps the reward of his victory; and in proportion as he reaps that reward fear is overcome. Our primary fear being fear of matter, much is gained by grasping the fact which modern science for the past ten or fifteen years has been carefully putting before us—vainly as far as most of us are concerned—that what we call matter is a force subject to the control of mind, while the directing of mind rests wholly with ourselves. Since we have controlled matter to make it in so many ways a hostile force, it ought to be within our power to turn it in our favour.

VIII

Which is, I suppose, the trend we are following, even if we follow it unconsciously. For the turning of the matter in our favour we have fortunately some notable examples. Our race has produced one perfectly normal man to whom all of us sub-normals can look as the type of what we are one day to become.

I think it a pity that so much of our thought of Him makes Him an exception to human possibilities. In speaking of Him as the Son of God we fancy Him as being in another category from ourselves. We forget that we, too, are sons of God—"heirs of God and co-heirs with Christ."[19] It is true that He realised that Sonship to a degree which we do not; but it is also true that we ourselves realise it to some degree. In the detail of the mastery of matter to which we shall attain it is fair, I think, to take Him as our standard.

Taking Him as our standard we shall work out, I venture to think, to the following points of progress.

a. The control of matter in furnishing ourselves with food and drink, by means more direct than at present employed, as He turned water into wine and fed the multitudes with the loaves and fishes.

b. The control of matter by putting away from ourselves, by methods more sure and less roundabout than those of to-day, sickness, blindness, infirmity, and deformity.

c. The control of matter by regulating our atmospheric conditions as He stilled the tempest.

d. The control of matter by restoring to this phase of existence those who have passed out of it before their time, or who can ill be spared from it, as He "raised" three young people from "the dead" and Peter and Paul followed His example.

e. The control of matter in putting it off and on at will, as He in His death and resurrection.

f. The control of matter in passing altogether out of it, as He in what we call His Ascension into Heaven.

IX

It will be observed that I take as historic records the statements of the Bible. This I do in face of the efforts of many of the clergy in a number of the churches to make me see in the Old Testament chiefly a collection of myths, and in the New a series of compilations by irresponsible hands, of doubtful date and authority, leaving, in the case of our Lord, only a substratum which can be relied on as biographical.

As an instance of what I mean I quote the following: A few weeks ago I happened to mention to the distinguished head of one of the most important theological schools of one of the largest denominations in the country, our Lord's turning the water into wine. "I've no idea that He ever did anything of the kind," were the words with which he dismissed the subject, which I did not take up again. I am not arguing here against his point of view. I merely state that I do not share it, and for these two main reasons:

First, because the so-called Higher Criticism on which it is based is a purely evanescent phase of man's learning, likely to be rejected to-morrow by those who accept it to-day, as has been the case with other such phases;

Secondly, because I feel sure that, with the mastery of matter to which we have already attained, the future development of our race will justify these seeming "miracles," and make them as natural and commonplace as telegraphy and telephony.

I speak only for myself when I say that the more I can feel round me the atmosphere of omnipotence the less I am aware of fear. It is a matter of course that the one should exclude the other. The sense of being myself, in a measure, the inheritor of omnipotence, as an heir of God and a co-heir with Christ, becomes, therefore, one to cultivate. This I can do only in proportion as I see that my Standard and Example cultivated it before me. In my capacity as a son of God I take as applying to myself the words reported by St. John: "In most solemn truth I tell you that the Son can do nothing of Himself—He can only do what He sees the Father doing; for whatever He does, that the Son does in like manner."

While sayings like these, of which there are many in the New Testament, apply doubtless, in the first place, to Him who best exemplifies the Sonship of God, they must apply, in the second place, I suppose, to all who exemplify that Sonship to any degree whatever. Man is the Son of God; and it is worth noting that He who is specially termed the Son of God is also specially termed the Son of Man. "Dear friends," St. John writes, elsewhere, "we are now God's children, but what we are to be in the future has not been fully revealed to us." I take it, therefore, as no presumption on my part to emphasise in my daily thought my place as a co-heir with Christ, feeling that not only is God's almightiness exercised on my behalf, but that as much of it as I know how to use is placed in my hands.

X

This last, of course, is very little. Even that little I use doubtfully, timidly, tremblingly. That is the utmost reach to which present race-development and personal development have brought me. With regard to the opportunities all round me I am as if I stood beside an airship in which I could fly if I knew how to work its engines, which I do not. Other conveniences besides airships would be of no good at all to me if someone more skilful than I didn't come to my aid. There is probably no person living of whom the same is not true. Large portions of omnipotence are placed within hands which are too busy grasping other things to seize all that they could hold.

I remember the encouragement it was to me when I understood that to hold anything at all was so much to the good as a starting-point. I had been in the habit of dwelling on the much I had missed rather than on the little I had apprehended. But the little I had apprehended was, after all, my real possession, and one I could increase. It is like the few dollars a man has in a savings bank. That at least is his, notwithstanding the millions he might have possessed if he had only known how to acquire them. There are many instances of a few dollars in the savings bank becoming the seedling of millions before the span of a man's life is passed.

To be glad of what we can do while knowing it is only a portion of what will one day be done is to me a helpful point of view. "There may be truth in all this," is the observation of a young lady who has scanned what I have written, "and yet I don't believe that we shall ever conquer fear." That, it seems to me, is to tie chains and iron weights about one's feet when starting on a race. If we are to keep in the race at all, to say nothing of winning it, the spirit must be free. One must add the courage which springs from a partial knowledge of the truth to the patience one gets from the understanding that as yet our knowledge of the truth is but partial.

XI

I often think that if the churches could come to this last admission it would be a help to themselves and to all of us. As already hinted I am anxious to keep away from the subject of churches through a natural dread of bitterness; but this much I feel at liberty to say, saying it as I do in deep respect for the bodies which have kept alive the glimmer of Divine Light in a world which would have blown it out. In a partially developed race the churches can have no more than a partially developed grasp of truth. A partially developed grasp of truth is much—it is pricelessly much—but it is not a knowledge of the whole truth. Not being a knowledge of the whole truth it should be humble, tolerant, and eager to expand.

The weakness of the ecclesiastical system strikes me as lying in the assumption, or practical assumption, on the part of each sect that it is the sole repository of truth, and of all the truth. There is no sect which does not claim more than all mankind can claim. Moreover, there is no sect which does not make its claims exclusively, asserting not only that these claims are right, but that all other claims are wrong. To the best of my knowledge, the sect has not yet risen which would make more than shadowy concessions to any other sect.

True, it must not be forgotten that no sect bases its teaching on what it has worked out for itself, but on the revelation made to it in Jesus Christ. Every sect would admit that its own view of truth might have been partial were it not for the fact that in Jesus Christ it has everything. Where the theories of men might be inadequate His immense knowledge comes in as supplementary.

This might be so had He Himself undertaken to give more than a partial view of truth. But He says expressly that He does not. He gives what His hearers might be assumed to be able to assimilate; but that is all. "I have much more to say to you, but you are unable at present to bear the burden of it."[20] It being an axiom in teaching to give the pupil only what he can receive, this is the utmost that our Lord attempts.

He goes on, however, to add these words, which are significant: "But when He has come—the Spirit of Truth—He will guide you into all the truth."[21] No doubt that process is even now going on, and will continue to go on in proportion as our race develops. We are being guided into all the truth, through all kinds of channels, spiritual, literary, scientific, philosophical. The naïve supposition that this promise was kept on the Day of Pentecost, when a sudden access of knowledge committed all truth to the apostles and through them to the Church forevermore, is contradicted by the facts. The apostles had no such knowledge and made no claims to its possession. The Church has never had it, either. "All truth" covers much more ground than do questions of ecclesiastical forms of government or of the nature of the sacraments. "All truth" must go as far as the Universal goes, leaving nothing outside its range. "All truth" must surely be such self-evident truth as to admit of no further dissensions.

Taking truth as a circle, the symbol of perfection, we may assume that our Lord disclosed a view of a very large arc in its circumference. But of the arc which He disclosed no one group of His followers has as yet perceived the whole. At the same time it is probable that each group has perceived some arc of that arc, and an arc perceived by no other group. "All truth" being too large for any one group to grasp, the Baptist sees his segment, the Catholic his, the Methodist his, the Anglican his, the Congregationalist his, until the vision of Christ is made up. I name only the groups with which we are commonly most familiar, though we might go through the hundreds of Christian sects and agree that each has its angle from which it sees what is visible from no other. Though there is likely to be error in all such perceptions a considerable portion of truth must be there, or the sect in question would not survive. It is safe to say that no sect comes into existence, thrives, and endures, unless it is to supply that which has been missed elsewhere.

XII

What place is there then for intersectarian or ecclesiastical arrogance?

The question is far from foreign to my subject. Fear is what arrogance feeds upon; fear is what arrogance produces; and arrogance is the special immorality of churches. To my mind the churches are almost precluded from combating fear, for the reason that arrogance is to so marked a degree their outstanding vice.

The Catholic is arrogant toward the Protestant; the Protestant is arrogant toward the Catholic; the Anglican is arrogant to him whom he calls a Dissenter in England, and merely "unchurches" in America; the Unitarian is arrogant to those whom he thinks less intellectual than himself; those who believe in the Trinity are arrogant toward the Unitarian. All other Christian bodies have their own shades of arrogance, entirely permitted by their codes, like scorn of the weak to the knights of Arthur's court. An active, recognised, and mutual arrogance all round is the reason why it is so rare to see any two or three or half a dozen Christian sects work for any cause in harmony. Arrogance begets fear as surely and prolifically as certain of the rodents beget offspring.

Much has been written during the past fifty years on the beautiful theme of the reunion of Christendom. Rarely does any great synod or convention or council meet without some scheme or some aspiration toward this end. Every now and then a programme is put forth, now by this body, now by that, with yearning and good intentions. And in every such programme the same grim humour is to be read behind the brotherly invitation. "We can all unite—if others will think as we do." Is it any wonder that nothing ever comes of these efforts? And yet, I am persuaded, a day will dawn when something will.

XIII

"When he has come—the Spirit of Truth—he will guide you into all the truth." That will be in the course of our race-development. As step is added to step, as milestone is passed after milestone, as we see more clearly what counts and what doesn't count, as we outgrow childishness, as we come more nearly to what St. Paul calls "mature manhood, the stature of full-grown men in Christ,"[22] we shall do many things that now seem impossible. Among them I think we shall view intersectarian arrogance as a mark of enfeebled intelligence. There will come an era of ecclesiastical climbing down. We shall see more distinctly our own segment of the arc which our Lord has revealed, and because of that we shall know that another man sees what we have missed. The Methodist will then acknowledge that he has much to learn from the Catholic; the Catholic will know the same of the Baptist; the Anglican of the Presbyterian; the Unitarian of the Anglican; and a co-operative universe be reflected in a co-operative Church. Each will lose something of his present cocksureness and exclusiveness. God will be seen as too big for any sect, while all the sects together will sink out of sight in God.

In the meantime we are only working toward that end, but toward it we are working. Every man who believes in a church is doing something to bring that end about when he gives a kindly thought to any other church. I say this the more sincerely owing to the fact that I myself am naturally bigoted, and such kindly thought does not come to me easily. There are sects I dislike so much that my eyes jump from the very paragraphs in the newspapers which mention them. And yet when I curb myself, when I force myself to read them, when I force myself to read them sympathetically and with a good wish in my heart, my mental atmosphere grows wider and I am in a stronger, surer, steadier, and more fearless world.

Much criticism has been levelled at the Church within the past few years; but it should be remembered that the Church no more than government, no more than business, no more than education, can be ahead of the only partially developed race of which she is one of the expressions. She is not yet out of the world of matter, though she is emerging. In proportion as her concepts, hopes, and aims remain material she will be as incompetent as any other body with the same handicaps and limitations. In proportion as she learns to "overthrow arrogant reckonings and every stronghold that towers high in defiance of the knowledge of God,"[23] she will become the leader of the world, and our great deliverer from fear.

XIV

B. Of the trials brought upon us by a world of men perhaps our chief resentment springs from their unreasonableness. They are not necessary; they might be avoided; at their worst they could be tempered. For this reason, too, they take us by surprise. Those who bring them on us seem captious, thoughtless, cruel. When they could so easily offer us a helping hand they obstruct us for the mere sport of doing so. People toward whom we have never had an unkindly thought will often go out of their way to do us a bad turn.

I shall not enlarge on this, since most of us are in a position to enlarge on it for ourselves. There is scarcely an individual for whom the way, hard enough at any time, has not been made harder by the barbed wire entanglements which other people throw across his path. Almost anything we plan we plan in the teeth of someone's opposition; almost anything with which we try to associate ourselves is fraught with discords and irritations that often inspire disgust. The worlds in which co-operation is essential, from that of governmental politics to that of offices and homes, are centres of animosities and suspicions, and therefore breeding-grounds of fear.

I suppose most grown-up people can recall the wounded amazement with which they first found themselves attacked by someone to whom they were not conscious of ever having given cause. Some are sensitive to this sort of thing; some grow callous to it; some are indifferent; and some are said to enjoy it. In the main I think we are sensitive and remain sensitive. I have been told by a relative of one of the three or four greatest living writers of English that the unfavourable comment of a child would affect him so that he would be depressed for hours. Statesmen and politicians, I understand, suffer far more deeply in the inner self than the outer self ever gives a sign of. The fact that our own weakness or folly or recklessness or wrong-doing lays us open to a blow is not much consolation when it falls.

XV

For myself all this became more tolerable when I had fully grasped the fact that we are still to a considerable degree a race of savages. From savages one cannot expect too much, not even from oneself. We have advanced beyond the stage at which one naturally attacked a stranger simply because he was a stranger, but we have not advanced very far. The instinct to do one another harm is still strong in us. We do one another harm when it would be just as easy, perhaps easier, to do one another good. Just as the Ashanti hiding in the bush will hurl his assegai at a passer-by for no other reason than that he is passing, so our love of doing harm will spit itself out on people just because we know their names.

Personally I find myself often doing it. I could on the spur of the moment write as many as twenty names of people of whom I am accustomed to speak ill without really knowing much about them. I make it an excuse that they are in the public eye, that I don't like their politics, or their social opinions, or their literary output, or the things they do on the stage. Anything will serve so long as it gives me the opportunity to hurl my assegai as I see them pass. One does it instinctively, viciously, because like other semi-savages one is undeveloped mentally, and it is to be expected.

By expecting it from others half our resentment is forestalled. Knowing that from a race such as ours we shall not get anything else we learn to take it philosophically. If I hurl my assegai at another, another hurls his assegai at me, and in a measure we are quits. Even if, trying to rise above my inborn savagery, I withhold my assegai, it is no sign that another will withhold his, and I may be wounded even in the effort to do my best. Very well; that, too, is to be expected and must be taken manfully.

The learning to take it manfully is what as individuals we get out of it. For the most part we are soft at heart, soft, I mean, not in the sense of being tender, but in that of being flabby.

On myself this was borne in less than a year ago. I had for some months been working hard at a picture-play which when put before the public was largely misunderstood. While some of the papers praised it others criticised it severely, but whether they praised or blamed I was seen as "teaching a lesson," a presumption from which I shrink. It is not that there is any harm in teaching a lesson if a man is qualified, but I no longer consider myself qualified. Sharing ideas is one thing, and the highest pleasure of the reason; but the assumption that because you suggest an idea you seek to convert is quite another thing. If I failed to make it plain that in this present book I was merely offering ideas for inspection, and in the hope of getting others in return, I should put it in the fire.

My picture-play once handed over to the public I experienced an intense reaction of depression. To figure through the country, wherever there are screens, as "teaching a lesson" seemed more than I could bear. It was more than I could bear, till it flashed on me that I couldn't bear it merely because I was inwardly flabby. I was not taking the experience manfully. I was not standing up to it, nor getting from it that toughening of the inner fibre which it had to yield. As usual in my case, owing to an acquaintance with the Bible imparted to me in childhood, a suggestion from the Bible was that which righted me again toward cheerfulness. It came, as such things always do, without any seeking, or other operation beyond that of the subconscious self.

Thou therefore endure hardness, as a good soldier of Jesus Christ.[24]

It was exactly what I needed to do—to endure hardness—to take it—to bear it—to be more of a man for it. Moreover, the idea was a new suggestion. I had not understood before that to the conquest of fear the hardening of the inner man is an auxiliary. My object had been to ward off fear so that it shouldn't touch me; but to let it strike and rebound because it could make no impact was an enlarging of the principle. Viewing the experience as a strengthening process enabled me not only to go through it but to do so with serenity.

This, I imagine, is the main thing we are to get out of the struggle brought on us through living in a world of men such as men are to-day. It is a pity they are not better, but being no better than they are we can get that much from the fact—the inner hardening. When, justly or unjustly, others attack or hurt or worry or anger or annoy me, the knowledge that through the very trial I am toughening within, where so often I am without moral muscle, can be a perceptible support.

XVI

C. Of the two main trials we bring on ourselves I suppose it would be only right to put sickness first.

Under sickness I include everything that makes for age, decay, and the conditions commonly classed as "breaking up." It is becoming more and more recognised, I think, that physical collapse has generally behind it a mental cause, or a long series of mental causes too subtle for tabulation.

I shall not dwell on this, for the reason that during the past fifty years so much has been written on the subject. A number of movements for human betterment have kept the whole idea in the forefront of the public mind. It is an idea only partially accepted as yet, arousing as much opposition among the conservative as hope on the part of the progressive. Since, however, science and religion are both, in their different ways, working on it together, some principle which can no longer be questioned is likely to be worked out within the next few generations.

All I shall attempt to do now is to re-state what seems to me the fact—stated by others with knowledge and authority—that God, rightly understood, is the cure of disease and not the cause of it. There is something repugnant in the thought of Universal Intelligence propagating harmful bacteria, and selecting the crises at which we shall succumb to their effects. The belief that God sends sickness upon us amounts to neither less nor more than that. The bacilli which we try to destroy He uses His almighty power to cultivate, so that even our efforts to protect ourselves become defiances of His Will.

Surely the following incident, which gives our Lord's attitude toward disease, affords a reasonable basis for our own.

"Once He was teaching on the Sabbath in one of the synagogues where a woman was present who for eighteen years had been a confirmed invalid; she was bent double, and was unable to lift herself to her full height. But Jesus saw her, and calling to her, He said to her, 'Woman, you are free from your weakness.' And He put His hands on her, and she immediately stood upright and began to give glory to God. Then the Warden of the Synagogue, indignant that Jesus had cured her on the Sabbath day, said to the crowd, 'There are six days in the week on which people ought to work. On those days therefore come and get yourselves cured, and not on the Sabbath day.' But the Lord's reply to him was, 'Hypocrites, does not each of you on the Sabbath day untie his bullock or his ass from the stall and lead him to water? And this woman, daughter of Abraham as she is, whom Satan had bound for no less than eighteen years, was she not to be loosed from this chain because it is the Sabbath day?' When He had said this all His opponents were ashamed, while the whole multitude was delighted at the many glorious things continually done by Him."[25]

It was not God, in His opinion, who had afflicted this woman; it was Satan, the personification of all evil. But in order that such references should not be misunderstood He had said of Satan, only a short time before, "I beheld Satan as lightning fall from heaven."[26]

Heaven, I take it, is creation as its Creator sees it. "God saw everything that he had made, and behold it was very good."[27] And from this creation, with the rapidity of the quickest thing we know anything about, a flash of lightning, our Lord saw the personification of evil blotted out. What thought had formed thought could destroy. The spectre which misunderstanding of God had raised in a life in which everything was very good became nothing at the instant when God was understood.

The occasion of His speaking the words I have quoted is worth noting as bearing on the subject.

A little earlier He had sent out seventy of His disciples to be the heralds of the Kingdom. "Cure the sick in that town, and tell them the Kingdom of God is now at your door."[28] By this time the seventy had returned, exclaiming joyfully, "Master, even the demons submit to us when we utter your name."[29] It was apparently the use of this word demons which called forth from Him that explanation, "I beheld Satan as lightning fall from heaven." In other words, Satan is the creation of wrong thought; the demons are the creations of wrong thought. Where the Universal Good is all there can be no place for evil or evil spirits. Banish the concept and you banish the thing. The action is as quick as thought, and thought is as quick as lightning. "I have given you power," He goes on to add, "to tread serpents and scorpions underfoot, and to trample on all the power of the Enemy; and in no case shall anything do you harm."[30]

This was no special gift bestowed on them and only on them. God has never, as far as we can see, dealt in special and temporary gifts. He helps us to see those we possess already. What our Lord seems anxious to make clear is the power over evil with which the human being is always endowed. It is probably to be one of our great future discoveries that in no case shall anything do us harm. As yet we scarcely believe it. Only an individual here and there sees that freedom and domination must belong to us. But, if I read the signs of the times aright, the rest of us are slowly coming to the same conclusion. We are less scornful of spiritual power than we were even a few years ago. The cocksure scientific which in its time was not a whit less arrogant than the cocksure ecclesiastical is giving place to a consciousness that man is the master of many things of which he was once supposed to be the slave. In proportion as the wiser among us are able to corroborate that which we simpler ones feel by a sixth or seventh sense, a long step will be taken toward the immunity from suffering which our Lord knew to be ideally our inheritance.

XVII

Sickness, age, decay, with all the horrors with which we invest our exit from this phase of existence, I take to be a misreading of God's intentions. We shall learn to read better by and by, and have already begun to do so. To this beginning I attribute the improvement which in one way or another has taken place in our general health—an improvement in which science and religion have worked together, often without perceiving the association—and in the prolonging of youth which in countries like the British Empire and the United States is, within thirty or forty years, to be noted easily.

Misreading of God's intentions I might compare to that misreading of his parent's intentions which goes on in the mind of every child of six or seven. He sees the happenings in the household, but sees them in a light of his own. Years afterwards, when their real significance comes to him, he smiles at his childish distortions of the obvious.

In comparison with what St. Paul calls "mature manhood, the stature of full-grown men in Christ," our present rating might be that of a child of this age. It is no higher. Misreading is all that we are equal to, but it is something to be able to misread. It is a step on the way to reading correctly. Though our impulse to learn works feebly it works restlessly; and a day will surely come when we shall be able to interpret God aright.

XVIII

Next to sickness I should place poverty as the second of the two great trials we bring upon ourselves.

Under poverty I class all sense of restriction, limitation, and material helplessness. As the subject will be taken up more in detail elsewhere I wish for the minute to say no more than this: that, in an existence of which Growth seems to be the purpose, God could not intend that any of us should be without full power of expansion.

What we are worth to him we must be worth as individuals; and what we are worth as individuals must depend on the peculiar combination of qualities which goes to make up each one of us. I, poor creature that I sometimes seem to others and always to myself, am so composed that God never before had anything exactly like me in the whole round of His creation. My value lies in a special blend of potentialities. Of the billions and trillions of human beings who have passed across this planet not one could ever have done what I can do, or have filled my place toward God and His designs.

Among the billions and trillions I may seem trivial—to men. I may even seem trivial to myself. To such numbers as these I can add so little when I come, and take away so little from them when I go, that I am not worth counting. Quite so—to all human reckoning. But my value is not my value to men; it is not even my value to myself; it is my value to God. He alone knows my use, and the peculiar beauty I bring to the ages in making my contribution. It is no presumptuous thing to say that He could no more spare me than any other father of a normal and loving family could spare one of the children of his flesh and blood.

Now, my value to God is my first reckoning. We commonly make it the last, if we ever make it at all; but it is the first and the ruling one.

What I am to my family, my country, myself, is all secondary. They determine only the secondary results. The first results come from my first relationship, and my first relationship is to God. As the child of my parents, as a citizen of my country, as a denizen of this planet, my place is a temporary one. As the son of God I am from everlasting to everlasting, a splendid being with the universe as my home.

Now this, it seems to me, is my point of departure for the estimate of my possible resources. I cannot expect less of the good things of the universe than God would naturally bestow on His son. To expect less is to get less, since it is to dwarf my own power of receiving. If I close the opening through which abundance flows it cannot be strange if I shut abundance out.

And that is precisely what we find throughout the human race, millions upon millions of lives tightly shut against His generosity. The most generous treatment for which the majority of us look is man's. The only standard by which the majority of us appraise our work is man's. You have a job; you get your twenty or thirty or fifty or a hundred dollars a week for it; and by those dollars you judge your earning capacity and allow it to be judged. You hardly ever pause to remember that there is an estimate of earning capacity which measures industry and good will and integrity and devotion, and puts them above all tricks of trade and rewards them—rewards them, I mean, not merely in mystical blessings in eons far off, possibly the highest blessings we shall ever know, but rewards them in a way that will satisfy you now.

"He satisfieth the empty soul," writes the psalmist, in one of the sublimest lyrics ever penned, "and filleth the hungry soul with goodness."

"Yes, of course," says the Caucasian. "When you have crushed out all your present cravings and forgotten them, He will give you joys of which now you have no conception."

But are not my present cravings those which count for me? and do they not make up precisely that character which renders me unique? True, my longings now may have to the longings I shall one day entertain only the relation of your little boy's craving for an alphabetic picture-book to the course in philosophy he will take when he is twenty-five; but so long as the picture-book is the thing he can appreciate you give it to him. Is not this common sense? And can we expect the Father of us all to act in other than common-sense ways?

It is because we do so expect—because we do so almost universally—that we have blocked the channels of His blessings. The world is crowded with men and women working their fingers to the bone, and even so just squeaking along betwixt life and death and dragging their children after them. They are the great problem of mankind; they rend the heart with pity. They rend the heart with pity all the more for the reason that there is no sense in their poverty. There is no need of it. God never willed it, and what God never willed can go out of life with the speed of Satan out of Heaven. We have only to fulfil certain conditions, certain conditions quite easy to fulfil, to find the stores of the Universal laid as a matter of course at the feet of the sons of God.

"Prove me now herewith, saith the Lord of Hosts," are the striking words of the prophet Malachi, "if I will not open you the windows of heaven and pour you out a blessing that there shall not be room enough to receive it.... And all nations shall call you blessed, for ye shall be a delightsome land,"

XIX

But it is the old story: we do not believe it. It is too good to be true, so we put it away from us. In a world where the material is so pressing we use only material measures, and bow only to material force.

So be it! That is apparently as far as our race-development takes us. It takes us into suffering, but not out of it. Individuals have come into it and worked their way out again; but most of us can go no faster than the crowd. In that case we must suffer. In a terrible crisis in his history, and after many sins, David was able to write these words: "I sought the Lord ... and He delivered me out of all my fears." It is the royal avenue, and it is open to anyone. And yet if we do not take it, it still does not follow that all is lost.

Of the world as it is the outstanding fact is the necessity for struggle. Struggle may conceivably enter into every other world. There is something in us which requires it, which craves for it. A static heaven in which all is won and there is nothing forevermore but to enjoy has never made much appeal to us. If eternal life means eternal growth we shall always have something with which to strive, since growth means overcoming.

While sorry, then, that we have not released ourselves to a greater degree than we have, we may take heart of grace from what we have achieved. We must simply struggle on. Struggle will continue to make and shape us. Whether our problems spring from a world of matter, from a world of men, or from ourselves, their solving brings us a fuller grasp of truth. The progress may be slow but it is progress. Hardship by hardship, task by task, failure by failure, conquest by conquest, we pull ourselves up a little higher in the scale. Some day we shall see in the Universal all that we have been looking for, and be delivered out of all our fears.

The World As It Is And The False God Of Fear

I

Of all fears the most dogging and haunting are those connected with money. Everyone knows them, even the rich. For many years I was their victim, and will now try to tell how I got rid of them so effectively that I may call it entirely.

Having a good many responsibilities I lived in terror of not being able to keep pace with their demands. The dread was like a malign invisible presence, never leaving me. With much in the way of travel, friendship, and variety of experience, which I could have enjoyed, the evil thing was forever at my side. "This is all very well," it would whisper in moments of pleasure, "but it will be over in an hour or two, and then you'll be alone with me as before."

I can recall minutes when the delight in landscape, or art, or social intercourse, became alien to me, something to be thrust away. Once in driving through rich, lush, storied Warwickshire on the way to Stratford-on-Avon—once in a great Parisian restaurant where the refinement, brilliancy, and luxury of the world seemed crushed into epitome—once at a stupendous performance of Götterdämmerung at Munich—once while standing on the shores of a lovely New Hampshire lake looking up at a mountain round which, as Emerson says, the Spirit of Mystery hovers and broods—but these are only remembered high points of a constant dread of not being able to meet my needs and undertakings. There used to be an hour in the very early morning—"the coward hour before the dawn," it is called by a poet-friend of my own—when I was in the habit of waking, only to hear the sleepless thing saying, as my senses struggled back into play, "My God, can you be sleeping peacefully, with possible ruin just ahead of you?" After that further sleep would become impossible for an hour or two, such wakings occurring, in periods of stress, as often as two and three times a week.

II

It was the spiritually minded man whom I have already quoted as giving me the three great points as to God's direction who first helped me to see that, on the part of anyone working hard and trying on the whole to do right, the fear of being left without means amounts in effect to denial of God. Thinking this over for myself during the course of some years, this fear has come to seem to me of the nature of blasphemy. It is like the "Curse God and die," of the wife of Job. I shall not hesitate to speak strongly on the subject, because so few are speaking on it strongly—while the urgency is pressing.

III

I have already said that it does not seem reasonable that the Father should put us into His universe to expand, and then deny us the power of expanding. The power of expanding is not wrapped up in money, but in the world as it is the independence of the one of the other is not very great. "One of the hardest things I ever had to do," a mother said to me, not long ago, "was to tell my little girl that her father and I could not afford to send her to college." That is what I mean. To most of us "expanding" and "affording" amount to the same thing.

True, there are natures which transcend the limitations of "affording," and by innate strength do what others resign themselves to not doing. For instance, there are men and women who "put themselves" through college, doing similar things which bring out the best in their characters. These are the exceptions; and they are the exceptions precisely for the reason that, whether they know it or not, they are nearer than their fellows to the divine working principle. It is not necessary for us to be conscious of that principle in order to get much of its result, though consciousness enables us to get more of it. The strong are strong because of harmony with God, at least to some extent. They may misuse their strength, as we can misuse anything; but the mere fact of possessing it shows a certain degree of touch with the Universal. But I am speaking chiefly of the weak, of those who think first of all in terms of restriction rather than in those of privilege to come and go and be and do.

I repeat that though this privilege is not dependent on money, money expresses it to the average mind.

And what is money after all? It is only a counter for what we call goods. Goods is the word with which, according to our Anglo-Saxon genius for the right phrase, we sum up the good things with which the Father blesses His children. The root connection between good, goods, and God is worth everyone's attention, A hundred dollars is simply a standard of measurement for so much of God's good things. A thousand dollars represents so much more; a million dollars so much more again. But it is important to note that this is not God's standard of measurement; it is man's, and adopted only for man's convenience.

As for God's standard of measurement it is inconceivable that the Universal Father should give to one of His children far more of His "goods" than he can use, while denying to another that which he is in absolute need of. The Universal Father could surely not do otherwise than bless all alike. With His command of resources He must bless all alike, not by depriving anyone, but by enriching everyone. If everyone does not enjoy plenty it must be because of the bringing in of some principle of distribution which could never have been His.

IV

The right and the wrong principles of distribution are indirectly placed before us by our Lord in one of the most beautiful passages which ever fell from human lips. Familiar as it is, I venture to quote it at length, for the reason that the modern translation makes some of the points clearer than they are in the King James version which most of us know best.

"No man can be the bondservant of two masters; for either he will dislike one and like the other, or he will attach himself to one and think slightingly of the other. You cannot be the bondservants both of God and of gold. For this reason I charge you not to be over-anxious about your lives, inquiring what you are to eat or what you are to drink, nor yet about your bodies, inquiring what clothes you are to put on. Is not the life more precious than its food, and the body than its clothing? Look at the birds which fly in the air; they do not sow or reap or store up in barns, but your Heavenly Father feeds them; are you not of much greater value than they? Which of you by being over-anxious can add a single foot to his height? And why be anxious about clothing? Learn a lesson of the wild lilies. Watch their growth. They neither toil nor spin, and yet I tell you that not even Solomon in all his magnificence could array himself like one of these. And yet if God so clothes the wild herbage which to-day flourishes and to-morrow is cast into the oven, is it not much more certain that he will clothe you, you men of little faith? Do not even begin to be anxious, therefore, saying, 'What shall we eat?' or 'What shall we drink?' or 'What shall we wear?' For all these are questions that Gentiles are always asking; but your Heavenly Father knows that you need these things—all of them. But make His Kingdom and righteousness your chief aim, and then these things shall be given you in addition. Do not be over-anxious, therefore, about to-morrow, for to-morrow will bring its own cares. Enough for each day are its own troubles."

In this passage there are two points, each of which may merit a few words as a means of eliminating fear.

V

The first point is the reference to what we are to make our "chief aim"—the Kingdom of God and righteousness.

I feel sure we generally miss the force of these words through our Caucasian sanctimoniousness. We can think of God's Kingdom and righteousness only in the light of the pietistic. The minute they are mentioned we strike what I have already called our artificial pose, our funereal frame of mind. I am not flippant when I say that in the mind of the Caucasian the first step toward seeking the Kingdom of God and righteousness is in pulling a long face. We can hardly think of righteousness except as dressed in our Sunday clothes, and looking and feeling wobegone. To most of us the seeking of righteousness suggests at once an increase in attending church services, or going to prayer-meetings, or making missionary efforts—excellent practices in themselves—according to the form of pietism we are most familiar with. Those of us who have no form of pietism feel cut off from making the attempt at all.

Oh, to be simple!—to be natural!—to be spontaneous!—to be free from the concept of a God shut up within the four walls of a building and whose chief interests are the sermon and the number of parishioners! The Kingdom of God is the Universal Kingdom, including everyone and everything—all interests, all commerce, all government, all invention, all art, all amusement, all the staid pursuits of the old and all the ardour of the young, all sport, all laughter, all that makes for gladness. It is the Kingdom of the bird and the flower and the horse and the motor-car and the motion-picture house and the office and the theatre and the ballroom and the school and the college and everything else that man has evolved for himself. He has evolved these things wrongly because nine times out of ten he has seen them as outside God's Kingdom, instead as being God's own undertakings because they are ours. All that we have to do to seek His Kingdom is to do what we are doing every day, with energy and fun, but to do it knowing we are His agents and co-workers. As a matter of fact, most of us are, to some extent, doing that already, getting food, shelter, clothing, and all other necessary things as our reward. What we do not get is relief from fear, because we do not understand that fear above all things is what He would take away from us.

VI

The second point is a curious one, and all the more emphatic for being curious. Our Lord invents a false god. He names the false god of fear, who was never named before. Mammon is the word which the modern translator gives as gold. As Mammon it is translated in the Authorised Version, whence we get the familiar phrase, "Ye cannot serve God and Mammon."

But Mammon was never the name of an idol or other form of false deity. The word, which is Syriac, means money. Our Lord, apparently, made it the name of a false god in order to set before us, and make vivid to us, a false principle.

That false principle is in the belief that the material essentials for living and expanding are dependent on man's economic laws.

This is a point of vast importance to the individual who desires to strike out beyond the crowd, not only getting what he needs, but ridding himself of fear.

The law of supply and demand is the most practical which the human race in its present stage has been able to evolve. That it is not an ideal law is obvious. There are ways in which it works, and ways in which it does not. When the Christians began to act for themselves they established a community of goods, such as had obtained among the little band who gathered round our Lord. Almost at once it was given up, presumably as being too advanced for the existing world of men. I suppose we might say the same of the various systems of Socialism and Communism urged on us at the present day. However good they may be, we are not ready to put them into practice. That, I judge—without positively knowing—is the reason why certain great Christian bodies oppose both. These bodies, I assume, are not hostile to equal distribution in itself, but only to equal distribution before men are developed to a stage at which it would be wise.

But my point is independent of all men's theories, and rests simply on the fact that, whatever the law of man, God is not bound by it.

If we can believe the Old and New Testaments—which, of course, some of us do not—He has shown on many, many occasions that He is far from being bound by it. Time after time He comes to the individual's relief according to His own law. We reject these occurrences as mythical on the ground that the laws of supply and demand—and some other laws as law is understood by us—do not support them; and yet it is in the power of the individual to test the truth for himself.

That is one of the burdens of both Testaments. The individual is implored to see the only real system for the distribution of "goods" as God's. It is not expressed in that way, but that is what it comes to. God owns and disposes of everything. He has not put us into His Universe and left us to fend for ourselves. He follows us. He cares for us. Not one is forgotten or overlooked by Him. It is personal watching and brooding and defence. He is our Father, not merely for the purpose of hearing us sing hymns, and forgiving our sins when we stop committing them, but for all our aims and objects. Nothing that concerns us is so small but that His Infinite Intelligence follows it; no need of ours is so large but that His All-Ownership can meet it. "Do not two sparrows sell for a half-penny?" is our Lord's illustration on this point, "yet not one of them will fall to the ground without your Father's leave. But as for you," He reasons, in order that we may understand the infinitesimal nature of God's care, "the very hairs on your heads are all numbered. Away then with fear!"[31]

VII

Away then with fear, because our first and over-ruling and all-determining relationship is to Him.

In eliminating money-fears from my own life that was the fact which helped me most. I had not only to seize it intellectually, but to get what William James calls the "feeling" of it, the apprehension of it in my subconsciousness. It was like acquiring a new instinct. The Metanoia, the re-directing of my thought, was a thorough and basic change.

It meant getting up in the morning with a new conception as to why I was working and for whom. I had taken it for granted hitherto that I was working for such and such a firm, for as much money as they would pay me. As much money as they would pay me was the limit of my expectation. Beyond the law of supply and demand I had no vision; and whenever the demand fell short fear was the result.

The change in my base was in seeing that working for such and such a firm, for as much money as they would pay me, was merely incidental. It was secondary. It was not what determined my position. It was not what determined my reward. It was a small way of looking at a situation which was big. It was a small way of looking at a situation which was big, merely to confine my objective to such selling and buying as goes on in the planet called the Earth. I was working for the Master of the Universe, who had all the resources of the universe with which to pay me for what I was worth to Him.

VIII

It is this last fact, as I have hinted already, which fixes my true value. To the firm for which I am working I am worth so many dollars and cents, and if for any reason I am unable to do their work they will get someone else who can. I am not essential to them in any way, however essential they may be to me. It is my part to "keep my job," since if I don't I may find it hard to get another. If I do get another it will be on the same principle, of being paid what I can be made to work for, and not a penny more.

But in working for the Master of the Universe I am working for One to whom I am essential. My "job" could not be "swung" by anyone else, since everyone else is essential to the swinging of his own. I am not "taken on" to do what anyone else could do as well; I am positively needed for this thing and for no other thing.

The nature of "this thing" for which I am needed may be seen in the obvious duties of my situation—as regards my family, my employers, and my surroundings, which sum up my responsibilities toward men in general. No explanation of myself can be independent of men in general, since my work is for them in its final aim. If I forget them I forget God, God expressing Himself to me through men in general, as through my family and my employers in particular.

Incidentally, then, I work for men, but essentially and consciously I work for God, and look to God for my recompense.

Now God is the most generous of all paymasters. It is natural enough that He should be so. He who delights in the grace of a bird or the colour of a flower must delight in a man in proportion to a man's higher place in the creative scale. As our Lord points out, that is no more than common sense. And, delighting in us as He does, God could not possibly stint us in what we earn from Him. Merely to suppose so is to dishonour Him. A large part of His joy must be in our joy.

The simplest way in which I can express it is that in consciously trying to work with God, not man, as our employer, things happen to us which, to the best of our foresight, would not have happened otherwise. Often they seem accidental, and possibly we ascribe them to accident till the coincidences become too numerous to explain by coincidence and nothing more. It constantly happens to myself, for instance, to find the whole solution of some tangled financial problem hanging on the chance turning of my steps to someone's office, and the chance turning of the conversation to some specific observation. Chance is the explanation which comes to me first, till I reflect on the finespun chain which brought me to that particular spot and those particular words. Leading is what I see then; and seeing it once I am more confident of being led the next time. The next time, therefore, I am the less afraid, having the definite experience to support me.

There are millions of men and women to whom life brings no more than the monotony of a treadmill round, year in and year out, with a cramping of mind, spirit, and ambition, who might have been free had they measured themselves by God's standards and not by men's. It is simply the taking of a point of view, and adjusting the life to it. In doing one's work primarily for God, the fear of undue restriction is put, sooner or later, out of the question. He pays me and He pays me well. He pays me and He will not fail to pay me. He pays me not merely for the rule of thumb task which is all that men recognise, but for everything else I bring to my job in the way of industry, good intention, and cheerfulness. If the Lord loveth a cheerful giver, as St Paul says, we may depend upon it that He loveth a cheerful worker; and where we can cleave the way to His love there we find His endless generosity.

In my own case this generosity has most frequently been shown in opening doors for me where I saw nothing but blank walls. He has made favourable things happen. It may be said that they would have happened anyhow; but when they have happened on my looking to Him, and have not happened when I did not look to Him, it is only fair to draw the conclusion that He was behind the event.

IX

It may also be urged that if there was really a God who delighted in us He would make favourable things happen to us whether we looked to Him or not. So He does. Every life, even among those who never think of Him, is full of such occurrences. Every individual gets some measure of supply for his necessities, and in many instances a liberal one. God's sun rises on the wicked as well as on the good, and His rain falls on those who do right and those who do wrong.

At the same time there is a force generated by working consciously with Him which we have to go without when we disregard Him. It is not, I suppose, that He refuses to co-operate with us, but that it is out of our power to co-operate with Him. If His is the only right way to our success and prosperity, and we are, to any extent, taking the wrong, it stands to reason that to that extent we must fail.

It is doubtless for this reason that our Lord emphasises seeking His righteousness as well as His Kingdom. His Kingdom might be roughly defined as His power; righteousness as the right way of doing anything. But you never obtain power by going the wrong way to work; whereas by working in the right way you get your result. The conclusion is obvious.

X

It is often objected to the point of view I have been trying to express that so much weight is thrown on material blessing. God gives spiritual rewards, it is contended, not material ones. To expect the material from Him is to make Him gross, and to become gross ourselves.

And yet those who put forth this objection are doing their utmost to secure material comforts, and to make material provision for the future. Are they doing it independently of God? Are they working in a medium into which God cannot enter? Is it argued for a single minute that "goods" are not God's good things, and that money is not their token? True, the love of money is the root of all evil. Of course—when you separate money from God, as Caucasians mostly do; not when you take money as one of the material symbols for God's love toward his sons.

As a matter of fact, we dig a gulf between the material and the spiritual which does not exist. We have seen that modern physical science is showing us how near to spirit matter comes, while it is highly probable that further research will diminish even the slight existing difference between them. Matter may really be considered as our sensuous misreading of the spiritual. That is to say, God sees one thing; our senses see another. In the wild lily cited by our Lord our senses see a thing exquisite in form and colour; and yet, relatively speaking, it is no more than a distortion of what God beholds and delights in. It is a commonplace fact that, even within the limitations of the senses, our sense-faculties perceive few things, if anything, quite accurately. Matter may therefore be considered as our wrong view of what God sees rightly. Both for Him and for us the object is there; but it is there with higher qualities than we can appreciate or understand.

The situation is not unknown among ourselves. A picture by a great master hangs on a wall. Two men look at it—the one with an expert knowledge of painting, the other with none. The untrained eye will translate into daubs of colour and meaningless forms what the skilled understanding will perceive as a masterly setting forth of beauty. So the good things—the "goods"—with which God blesses us, as well as the money which is their symbol, may be taken as having to God a meaning which they do not possess for us, but not as being outside the sphere of His interest and control.

XI

It is the tendency to puts "goods" and money outside the sphere of His interest and control which has impelled us—and perhaps the Caucasian especially—to have one God for the spiritual and another for the material. We try to serve God and Mammon to an extent far beyond anything we are generally aware of. It is not merely the individual who is doing it; it is part of our collective, social, and national life. Our civilisation is more or less based on the principle.

It is a mistake to suppose that a formal belief in One Almighty, All-knowing, All-loving God has, to the immense majority of us, ever been more than an ideal. It is a mistake to suppose that because the false god is no longer erected before us in silver or stone he is no longer served. The world has never outgrown idolatry, the so-called Christian world no more than any other. "Dear children," are the words with which St. John closes one of his epistles, "guard yourselves from idols." He at least did not think that the idol had been forsaken because the use of his name was given up.

We may define as a god any force to which we ascribe a supreme and controlling power in our lives. It is of little consequence whether or not we give it name and personality, so long as that force rules us. So long, too, as it wields a power which the One God does not, so long as we make the false god greater than the true, and more influential.

This is no mere figure of speech; it is fact. We have never guarded ourselves from idols. We have never done more toward recognising the Father than the putting Him in the pantheon with our other gods. Even though we have inscribed the whole pantheon with His name, the other gods have been in it.

XII

I have said that our whole collective life is based on the principle of one God for the soul and another for the body; and so it is. In what we call our temporal life God gets only a formal recognition, while Mammon is the referee. Beyond the controlling power of money we have no vision, and we see no laws. The sphere of material productivity being one in which, according to our foregone conclusion, God does not operate, we have to make the controlling power of money our only practical standard. It has its laws—chiefly the laws of supply and demand—within whose working we human beings are caught like flies in spider-webs. Though we struggle, and know we are struggling, we take it for granted that there is nothing to do but struggle, and struggle vainly. We take it for granted that we are born into a vast industrial spider-web, whence there is no possibility of getting out, and in which we can only churn our spirits rebelliously. In proportion as God is a God of love, Mammon is a god of torture; but such is our supineness of spiritual energy that we go on serving Mammon.

XIII

But I am writing only for the individual. I am trying to suggest to him that however much his race, his nation, his society, may serve Mammon, he is free to renounce the idol and escape the idol's laws. Escaping the idol's laws he comes within the realm of God's laws; and coming within the realm of God's laws he reaches the region of plenty.

He may be the poorest and most ill-paid labourer; but God will recognise his industry not in proportion to its technical skill, but according to the spiritual excellence which goes into it. Technical skill depends largely on the right man finding the right job; but as our world is organised at present the right man, more often than not, is put into the wrong job and has to do his best with it.

God sees and estimates that best; and as surely as He makes His sun to rise and His rain to fall will give it its just compensation.

XIV

Our industrial questions are primarily spiritual. That is why they can never be settled on a purely economic basis, and why every attempt to settle them on a purely economic basis leads to conditions more confused than those from which we have emerged. The so-called purely economic basis is the basis where only Mammon's laws are considered, and God's are held to be impractical.

Quite so! But even then the individual is free. Working with God he is always master of the situation as it affects him.

The problem of Capital and Labour, for example, has, in one form or another, been before the world for thousands of years. The more acute it becomes the further we are from a solution, and were never so far from a solution as we are to-day. Poverty, again, is the canker at the heart of both Church and State, and has been so in every stage of our civilisation. In 1921 it is no more under control than it was in the days of Charlemagne or Attila or Xerxes. Charitable efforts to relieve it have proved as effective as tickling with a feather to cure disease. Or again, high prices and low wages, high wages creating high prices, resented conditions leading to strikes, strikes bringing confusion to both wages and prices alike—these things perplex the most clear-sighted among us, compelling us to wonder as to what new troubles we are heaping up. Or again, taxes crippling incomes and gnawing at the heart of industry vex us each year with a sense of the futility of all man's efforts for the common good, and the uselessness of our energies. These difficulties, with many kindred ones, are the working of the laws of Mammon. The case is simple. We shall never be free from the difficulties till we are free from the laws. The bondservants of Mammon will go on from misery to misery, till the will which opposes God is broken down. There is no other way. The colossal disintegration of the world now taking place before our eyes may be the beginning of this end.

XV

But I return to the point I have emphasised already, the only point to this book. The individual can act on his own account. He does not have to wait till the race as a whole gives up the service of Mammon, or even the nation to which he belongs. He can set himself free, and enjoy the benefits of freedom.

There must be many to whom, as to myself, the kingdom of heaven will really be at hand when they are delivered from the snares and entanglements of man's economic systems. Caught in those systems, imprisoned in them, more hopelessly enmeshed the more they struggle to save themselves, the suggestion that a change in point of view will take us out of them will seem to some of us too amazing to be true.

Nothing will prove it true but a man's own experience. Mine will convince nobody; no other man's can convince me. Demonstration must be personal before we can make anything our own. But the fact remains, as sure as the surest thing we know anything about, that the law of Mammon does not work, while the law of God does work, and will work for anyone who calls it to his aid.

No one who has ever seen the early morning trains into any great city vomiting forth their hundreds of thousands of men and women, trudging more or less dispiritedly to uncongenial jobs, can have felt anything but pity for so many lives squeezed into the smallest possible limitations. Admitting cheerfulness, admitting a measure of content, and a larger measure of acceptance of what can't be helped, there still remains over these hordes the shadow of a cloud from which they know they never will escape. Clerks, factory hands, tradesmen, working men and women of every stamp and occupation, they bow to the fact that they will always work hard at tasks which are rarely their own choice, that they will always work for little money, that they will always be denied their desires for expansion; that as it was with their fathers and mothers before them, so it will be with them, and so it will be with their children after them.

With the supineness of our race most of them force themselves to be satisfied with what comes. But here and there is a rebel. Here and there is a man or a woman who feels that joyless work, and small pay, and little or nothing to look forward to, are cruel elements in life, not fair, not just, on the part of God or man. But what can they do? They are in man's economic machine. The machine turns round and they turn with it. They can do nothing else but turn with it. They see no prospect except of turning with it till they die.

It is out of such men and women that our modern world breeds revolutionists, that exalted and yet dangerous band who seek redress from the laws of Mammon by appealing to the laws of Mammon, so making confusion worse confounded.

XVI

A revolution indeed is needed; but a revolution in point of view.

Political revolution, for the sake of righting governmental abuses, has been known to produce beneficent results.

Material revolution, the attack of the poor on the rich to take away their possessions, has never achieved anything. Many a time it has been tried, and many a time it has failed. Being part of the system of Mammon it could do nothing else than fail. The evils which Mammon has wrought Mammon will never remedy. There may be instances in history of economic cures for economic ills; but I think they are few. In general such cures are of the nature of our "settlements" of strikes. They settle to-day what is again unsettled to-morrow, leaving the work to be done all over again, and so on into a far future.

The revolution in point of view has these great advantages:

First, it contains within it the seeds of success, since it is revolution toward God, the owner of the Earth and the fulness thereof; Next, it takes place within the individual himself, doing no one else any harm;

Lastly, it does not run counter to man's economic laws; it only uses and transcends them. It directs and corrects them. Working along their lines it stimulates their fruit. Letting the inner man out of the economic trap it sets him in a world in which first, and last, and before everything else, he is God's servant in God's pay. God's pay being sure, and paid in the way we need it, we no longer have money-fear to be afraid of. Money-fear being set aside we can the more easily give ourselves to the knowledge that "the Kingdom of God does not consist of eating and drinking, but of right conduct, peace, and joy, through the Holy Spirit; and whoever in this way devotedly serves Christ, God takes pleasure in him, and men commend him highly."[32]

XVII

And lest what I have said should seem fanciful or chimerical let me add that I am not saying these things merely on my own responsibility. To my certain knowledge there are hundreds of thousands—some millions—of people throughout the world who at this very minute are living according to this principle, and proving that it works in practical effect.

Neither am I speaking theoretically, as I have tried to make plain. To a degree that convinces myself I have made the demonstration. Where my life was like a dark and crooked lane in which I might easily be lost, it has now become as an easy and open highway; where money-fear was the very air I breathed, it is now no more than a nebulous shred on a far horizon. Money-fear comes occasionally; but only as the memory of pain to a wound which you know to be healed. It comes; but, like Satan out of Heaven, I can cast it from me with a thought.

The False God Of Fear And The Fear Of Death

I

The fear of death was greatly diminished for me on grasping the principle of everlasting Growth.

This principle we gather from whatever we know of life. Our observation of life is, of course, limited to this planet; but as far as it goes it shows us a persistent and perpetual system of development. We have only to let our imaginations go back to the first feeble stirrings of life in the ooze of the primeval seas, contrasting that with what it became in Plato, Sophocles, St. Peter, St. Paul, Raphael, Shakespeare, and Darwin, to see how high the climb upward has reached. Jesus of Nazareth I put on a plane to which we have not yet attained, though in sight as the great objective.

II

That the same law operates in the individual life is a matter of everyone's experience. Such knowledge as each man has of himself is that of a growing entity. Each year, each day, expands him a little further, with increased fulness of character. At thirty he is more than he was at twenty; at fifty more than he was at thirty; at eighty more than he was at fifty. Nothing but a perverted mortal point of view stands in the way of further expansion still.

The perverted mortal point of view is one of the impulses we have to struggle with. The mortal tendency, which means the deadly tendency, always seeks to kill whatever has the principle of life. This tendency is in every one of us; but in some of us more than in others.

You can see it at work in the morbid mind, in the mind that is easily depressed, and in the mind that easily closes.

Perhaps it is in this last that it becomes our most pernicious enemy. The closing mind is found in all our ranks; the closed mind is the deadwood of all our professions. It is not only deadwood; it is death-in-life, the foe of the developing life-principle, the enemy of the Holy Ghost.

That the dead mind should be found among people who have had few intellectual advantages is not surprising. On them it is forced from without, by sheer pressure of circumstance. Where it is most painful is precisely where it does most harm, among the classes we call professional. There, too, it seems commonest. Lawyers, doctors, clergymen, teachers, writers, politicians, business men with dead minds choke all the highways of life. To the extent that they have influence they are obstacles to progress; but sooner or later the time comes when they no longer have influence. Life shelves them on the plea that they are old; but that is not the reason. They are shelved because they have killed their minds, becoming living dead men.

As a matter of fact, one of the most valuable of our social and national assets is the old man who has kept his mind open. Found all too rarely, he is never shelved, for the reason that life cannot do without him. Having the habit of expansion he continues to expand, keeping abreast of youth and even a little in advance of it. The exception rather than the rule, there is no reason why he should not be the racial type.

III

He is not the racial type because so many of us begin to die almost as soon as we have begun to live. Our very fear of the death-principle admits it into our consciousness. Admitted into our consciousness it starts its work of killing us. It wrinkles the face, it turns the hair grey, it enfeebles the limbs, it stupefies the brain. One of its most deadly weapons is fatigue, or the simulation of fatigue. The tired business man, who rules American life, is oftener than not a dead business man. If he looked ahead he would see what we idiomatically know as his "finish." He is not only dying but he infuses death into manners, literature, and art, since he so largely sets the standard which becomes the rule.

War on the death-principle should be, it seems to me, one of the aims to which the individual gives his strength; and once more he can do it on his own account.

In the first place, he can watch himself, that he does not mentally begin to grow old. To begin mentally to grow old is to begin mentally to die. He must think of himself as an expanding being, not as a contracting one. He must keep in sympathetic touch with the new, damning the know-it-all frame of mind. He must keep in sympathetic touch with youth, knowing that youth is the next generation in advance. The secrets of one generation are not those of another; but if he who possesses the earlier masters also the later he is that much the richer and wiser. The gulf which separates parents and children is one which the parents must cross. They can work onward, while the children cannot work backward. Up to a certain point the older teach the younger; beyond a certain point the younger teach the older. He who would go on living and not begin to die must be willing to be taught, reaping the harvest of both youth and age.

In the second place, he who would live must not kill anyone else. The deadly tendency in ourselves is forever at work on those about us, chiefly on those we love. We watch, tabulate, and recount their symptoms of decay. Making notes of them for ourselves we discourse of them to others. "He begins to look old," is a commonplace. The response will probably emphasise the fact. By response to response we spin round a friend the age-web which lengthens into the death-web. In our expressive American vernacular we speak of "wishing" conditions on others, an instinctive folk-recognition of the force of mentality. We do it in a sinister sense more often than by way of helpfulness. We "wish" by thinking, by talking, by creating an atmosphere, by forcing things into the general consciousness. Old age and decay, bad enough in themselves, we intensify by our habits of mind. Death, which in any case awaits our friends, we woo to them by anticipations of demise. It is not ill-intentioned. It comes out of a subconsciousness in which death and not life is the base.

IV

For most of us the fear of death is a subconscious rather than an active fear. It becomes active for those who through illness, or in some other way, see a sentence of death hanging over them; but during the greater part of the life-span we are able to beat it off.

As to the life-span itself there is reason to suppose that it is meant to be more regular than man allows it to become. There may easily be an "appointed time" to which we do not suffer ourselves, or each other, to attain. Those strange, inequalities by which one human being is left to pass over the century mark, another is cut off just when he is most needed, while a third does no more than touch this plane for an hour or two, may be the results of our misreadings of God's Will, and not the decrees of that Will itself.

We are here on ground which may be termed that of speculation; and yet speculation is not quite the right word. I dare to think that we have reached a stage of our development at which we are entitled to make with regard to death certain inferences which were hardly possible before our time. We may make them timidly, with all hesitation and reserve, aware that we cannot propound them as facts; and yet we may make them. The human mind is no longer where it was a hundred years ago, still less where it was five hundred years ago. Though we make little progress we make some. We are not always marking time on the same spot of ignorance and helplessness. What is mystery for one age is not of necessity mystery for another. Even when mysteries remain, they do not of necessity remain without some hint of a dawn which may broaden into day. Many of our most precious illuminations have come in just this way; a faint light—which slowly, feebly, through centuries perhaps, waxes till it becomes a radiance.

V

I talked some time ago to an orthodox Christian lady whose brother had recently died, and who was speaking of death.

"The one mystery," she called it, "on which no single ray of light has been vouchsafed in all the ages man has been on earth."

I did not agree with her, but knowing her to be an orthodox Christian lady I did not venture to express my opinion.

But hers is the position which many, perhaps most, of us take. "No one has ever come back," we say, "to tell us what his experience has been," and we drop the subject there. Not only do we drop the subject there, but we resent it if everyone else does not drop the subject there. "God has hidden it from us," we declare, "and what He has hidden from us it is presumption for us to pry into." It is useless to urge the fact that this way of reasoning would have kept us still in the Stone Age; we are not to be reached by argument.

Let me say at once that I am not taking up the question of the psychic, or entering into it at all. I shall keep myself to the two points of view which have helped me, as an individual, to overcome, to some degree, the fear of death, considering them in reverse order from that in which I have mentioned them. Those two points of view are:

A. That, according to God's Will, we come into this phase of being for an "appointed time" which we do not always reach;

B. That we pass out of this phase of being as we came into it, for Growth.

VI

A. The question of an appointed time seems important chiefly to the right understanding of God's love. Between us and the understanding of that love bereavement is often a great obstacle. Oftener still it is a great puzzle. I do not have to catalogue the conditions in which the taking away of men, women, and children, sorely needed here if for no other purpose than to love, has moved us to deep perplexity, or to something like a doubt of God. We have probably all known cases where such tragedy has driven sufferers to renounce God altogether, and to curse Him. Some of us who have been smitten may have come near to doing this ourselves, or may have done it.

VII

I have already spoken of the Caucasian's habit of shuffling off on God those ills for which he will not face the responsibility himself, and I am inclined to think that this is one of them. In my own experience the explanation of "God's Will" made to the mother of a little family left fatherless, or to the parents of a dead baby, or to a young man with a young wife in her coffin, has always been revolting. I have made it; I have tried, on the faith of others, to think it must be so. I have long since ceased to think it, and feel happier for not crediting the Universal Father with any such futile tricks.

I should not go so far as to say that we human beings have misapplied the laws of life in such a way as to kill those who are dear to us; rather, I think, we have never learned those laws except in their merest rudiments. We are not yet prepared to do more than bungle the good things offered us on earth, and more or less misuse them. We misuse them ourselves; we teach others to misuse them; we create systems of which the pressure is so terrible that under it the weak can do nothing but die. We give them no chance. We squeeze the life out of them. And then we say piously, "The blessed Will of God!"

As an illustration of what I mean let me cite the two following cases among people I have known:

A young lady belonging to a family of means was found to be suffering from incipient tuberculosis. The doctors ordered her to Saranac. To Saranac she went, with two nurses. Within eighteen months she was home again, quite restored to health. This was as it should have been.

At the same time I knew a car-conductor, married some six or seven years, and the father of three children. He, too, was found to be suffering from incipient tuberculosis. He, too, was ordered to Saranac. But having a wife and three children to support, Saranac was out of the question. He went on conducting his car till his cough became distressing, whereupon he was "fired." A minimum allowance from his church kept the family from starvation, while the nearest approach to Saranac that could be contrived was an arrangement by which he slept with his head out the window. In course of time he died, and his widow was exhorted to submit to the Will of God.

VIII

I cite the latter case as typical of millions and millions of deaths of the kind at which we stand aghast at God's extraordinary rulings. Why is it, we ask, that He snatches away those who are needed, leaving those who might be spared? As to the latter part of the question I have nothing to say; but when it comes to "snatching away" I feel it important to "absolve God" of the blame for it.

In the instance I have quoted the blame for it is clear. Falling on no one individual, it does fall on an organisation of life which gives all the chances to some, denying them to others. So long as we feel unable to improve on this organisation we shall have these inequalities. But let us face honestly the consequences they bring. Let us not confuse all the issues of life and death as we do, by saddling the good and beautiful Will of God with the ills we make for ourselves.

IX

All untimely bereavement is, of course, not of the nature of the above illustration. And yet I venture to believe that in all untimely bereavement some similar explanation could be found. For example, in the intervals of writing these lines I have been reading a recent biography of Madame de Maintenon. In it is a chapter describing the series of catastrophes which fell on Louis the Fourteenth, and the French kingdom, within little more than a twelvemonth. His son and heir, his grandson, the second heir, his great-grandson, the third heir, the second heir's wife, and still another grandson were all carried off by smallpox. In the apartments of Madame de Maintenon, his wife, the aged monarch was counselled to submit to the awful Will of God which saw fit thus to smite him. What no one perceived was that by crowding round the bed of each sufferer in turn the survivors courted contagion.

But, there again, it is not much more than a century since this fact became known to anyone. Easily within living memory is the discovery that disease is due to bacteria. Our whole system of sanitation is of recent development, and obtains only among the English and the Americans even now. In many parts of Europe and America, to say nothing of Asia and Africa, people still live as in the Middle Ages, and infant mortality is appalling. Those of us who pay most attention to sanitary laws live unhealthily, diminishing our powers to resist attack. I mention these facts, not as making a list of them, but to indicate the many causes through which we bring bereavement on ourselves, when the Will of God would naturally make for survival and happiness.

It must never be forgotten that in this phase of our existence we never carry out that Will except to a remote degree. We only struggle towards doing it. When great sorrows come it is because in the struggle we have not been successful. Either we ourselves have failed; or the failure of others affects us indirectly. While God's Will may be for our happiness, we can attain to neither the happiness nor the Will—as yet.

Nevertheless, we would not have it otherwise. In our more thoughtless or more agonised minutes we are likely to cry out for a life in which the conditions ensuring our happiness could not so easily miscarry; but that would mean a static life, and a static life, above all things, we will not endure. As already seen, we ask for difficulties to conquer, successes to achieve. To contend is our instinct, not to be passive and enjoy.

Difficulties to conquer can only exist side by side with the possibility of not conquering them. The victory which is merely a walk-over is scarcely a victory. Achievement counts only when something has been overcome. Even then the overcoming of one thing merely spurs us on to overcome another. To rest on our laurels is doom. For a race which has the infinite as its goal the word must be on and on. The static heaven of bearing palms and playing harps and bliss, which the naïve interpretation of our fathers drew from the imagery of the Apocalypse, has long since made us rebellious. Something to strive for we demand, even at the risk of bereavement.

X

It is at once the disadvantage and the glory of our own generation that it is only on the fourth or fifth step of the stairway by which we are climbing. But at least it is heir to the conquests which go to its stage of advance. Untimely bereavement is less common to-day than it was a few centuries ago; it is more common to-day than it will be a few centuries hence. Such storms of affliction as in 1712 swept over the house of Louis Quatorze occur less frequently now. But they still occur. We have not got beyond them. They are only bound to occur less and less frequently, till they become no more than matters of scarcely credible record.

In the meanwhile it may be a comfort to others, as it is to me, to be able to "absolve God" from the charge of capricious and intolerable thwarting of our love. To me, at least, the blow is easier to bear when I know that His beloved hand didn't strike it. I cannot understand being tortured out of sheer love, while patience with what leaves me with my whole life maimed is only the patience of the vanquished.

On the other hand, I can bear with my mistakes, I can bear with the mistakes of others, I can bear with the failures which are the fruit of our lack of race-development, so long as I know that God is on my side. The affliction which would be too poignant as coming directly from Him is half soothed already when I know that He is soothing it. I may have lost what He gave; but far from snatching it from me He would have had me keep it. Of all my comforts that assurance is the first.

In addition, I have the satisfaction—a meagre satisfaction you may call it, but a satisfaction all the same—of knowing that by the ploughing and harrowing of my heart a step is taken toward that future in which hearts shall be less harrowed and ploughed. "It must never happen again." That is what we keep saying with regard to the Great War. Well, it may happen again. We have as yet no trustworthy pledge to the contrary. But of this we may be sure, that it will not happen again very often. It is less likely to happen again for the very reason that it has happened. If the Great War does not prove to be the last war it is the more probable that the next war will. I mean that we do learn our lessons, though we learn them only as feeble-minded children learn theirs. Agony by agony, something is gained, and my personal agony counts with the rest. The fact may give me no more than the faintest consolation, and possibly none at all; and still in the long, slow stages of our upward climb my agony counts, whether its counting consoles me or not.

XI

The inference that we come into the life of this planet for an "appointed time" we draw from what we see of God's system of order. All other things do so, as far as we observe. The plant springs, to grow and bloom, to bear fruit and seed, and so renew itself. Fish, bird, and animal have their appointed round varying only in detail from that of the plant. Man's appointed round would seem to vary only in detail from that of the animal, except that he himself interferes with it.

To the best of my knowledge the plant, from the blade of grass to the oak or the orchid, always fulfils its life-span, unless some act or accident cripples or destroys it. I mean that we never see God bringing the shoot above the soil just to nip it before it unfolds. We never see Him bring the bud to the eve of blossoming just to wither it. Having given it its mission He supplies it with rain, sun, and sustenance to bring that mission to its end. True, the plant has enemies, like everything else, enemies which it may not escape. But generally speaking, it does escape them, and lives to finish its task.

So, too, with the more active living thing. It, too, has its enemies. It, too, may not escape them. But assuming that it does, God allows it, to the best of our observation, to work out its full development. The only "bereavement" he brings to the lion, the thrush, or the elephant, or any other creature capable of grief is, apparently, from those hostile sources of which the hostility is more or less gratuitous. A man shoots a lion, or the lion kills an antelope; but they do so through misreading of God's Will, not through fulfilling it.

For the lower ranks of creation misread that Will in their way as much as the higher in theirs. All ferocity must be misinterpretation of the divine law of harmony and mutual help. Internecine destruction probably has a meaning we can only guess at. Guessing at it we are at liberty to surmise that what God sees as loving contention for excellence, each gaining by the other's gain, we understand as bitter strife, and consumption of the flesh and blood. The rivalry we can best appreciate is that of brutality; the chief benefit the stronger creature seeks from the weaker is in killing and eating him. Why this should be part of our struggle I do not know; but part of our struggle it seems to be—from the humblest organism up to man—the mistaking of God's Will before learning to understand it.

And lest I should seem to assume too much, in saying this, let me add that our progress out of this state of preying on each other has long been foreseen by the pioneers of truth. The vision is at least as ancient as Isaiah, when he descried from afar the accomplished rule of the Son of David:

"With righteousness shall he judge the poor, and reprove with equity for the meek of the earth.... And righteousness shall be the girdle of his loins, and faithfulness the girdle of his reins. The wolf also shall dwell with the lamb, and the leopard shall lie down with the kid; and the calf and the young lion and the fatling together; and a little child shall lead them. And the cow and the bear shall feed; their young ones shall lie down together.... And the sucking child shall play on the hole of the asp, and the weaned child shall put his hand on the adder's den. They shall not hurt nor destroy in all my holy mountain; for the earth shall be full of the knowledge of the Lord, as the waters cover the seas."

XII

If I am correct in thinking that our passage across the life of this planet is meant to last for an "appointed time," I presume that that time would be measured by experience rather than by years. There exists what we vaguely call the round of life. We are born; we grow; we know family interests; we learn; we work; we love; we marry; we beget children; we train them to take our places; we pass beyond. There are variations on this routine, some of us having more, some of us having less; but in general it may be taken as typical. It is our mission, as the plants and the lower living things have theirs.

It seems reasonable, then, to think that each baby born is meant by the Father's Will to reap this experience before it proceeds to further experience. It must be a stage in its growth or it would not come into it. When it is balked of it something is amiss. The child who dies in infancy has lost something. The lad or the girl whom our organised life drives from this plane before reaching fruition has lost something. The parent whom our conditions force onward before he has brought his task to a stage at which he can peacefully lay it down has lost something. I am not saying that God does not control resources by which that loss can be abundantly made up, but only that the loss would seem to be there. It is loss for the one who departs as well as for those who remain behind.

XIII

That is what I gather from the instances in the Old and New Testament in which those who had gone on before their time were called back again. There are six of these instances in all: one in the Old Testament, and five in the New. Of four of them we are expressly told that those restored were young; of the other two nothing is said as to age, but one at least was probably young, while the other was greatly needed.

The child called back by Elisha was still a little boy. The daughter of Jairus was still a little girl. The son of the widow of Nain was a young man, as was also Eutychus raised by St. Paul. Though we are not told the age of Lazarus we judge that he was at most no more than in man's maturity. Dorcas of Lydda may have been of any age, but, judging by the circumstances, she had not completed her task.

XIV

My point is this, that if these things happened, they seem to bear out my suggestion that our own inducement of premature death cuts us off from fulfilling our appointed time and getting our appointed experience. Only on some such ground can we believe that any would be permitted to return.

Should this be so we would be in a position to assume that all who go over ahead of time would be allowed to come back, if we had sufficient spiritual power to recall them. But that power is of the rarest. Our Lord, apparently, was in control of it only at times, and on at least one occasion, that of the raising of Lazarus, its exercise was not what we should call easy. But that He believed it to be at human command to some extent is clear from the fact that its use became one of His four basic principles. "Raise the dead," was the second of the commands with which He sent out his first seventy disciples.

XV

I dwell on the subject only because of its bearing on the love of God. If it becomes plain to us that by the understanding of God's Will we gain a richer experience, with less fear of being cut off before our work is done, that Will makes a stronger appeal for being understood. That we have not understood it earlier, that we have not particularly cared to understand it, is due, I think, to our assumption of its capriciousness. It has been so underscored as inscrutable—the word generally applied to it—that the man in the street has felt mystified by it from the start. Being mystified he has settled down to think as little about it as he could.

But a great force striving with man to put common sense into his methods is worth comprehending. It does not compel us to common-sense methods for the reason that we value only that which we work out for ourselves. We work nothing out but through suffering. We learn nothing, we take no forward step, except as we are whipped to it by anguish. That is why there is so much mourning in the world. God does not cause it; we bring it on ourselves; but each time we bring it on ourselves we creep one tiny step nearer that race-conclusion which is now coming to us about war, and will one day come to us about death, that "It must never happen again."

XVI

In other words, death will be abolished by race-unanimity not to submit to it. We shall have travelled far in this direction when the average mind begins to perceive that God did not send death into His creation, but that we ourselves developed it. Having developed it ourselves we must get rid of it ourselves, and already some of that work has been done. "For seeing that death came through man," are the words of St. Paul, "through man comes also the resurrection of the dead." When he speaks of "Jesus Christ who hath abolished death," his words are stronger still. "He has put an end to death and has brought Life and Immortality to light by the Good News, of which I have been appointed a preacher, apostle, and teacher."

This Life and Immortality are not to be relegated to other ages and worlds; they are for us to work out now.

The degree to which we work them out depends on our own efforts. Death will be our doom for many generations to come, because so few of us have the energy to strive against it. Release can come only when the race at large is willing to cast the evil thing off. One would suppose that we would be willing now; but we are far from being willing. We shall go on forcing our dear ones to die before their time, falling sick ourselves, enduring agonies, and rotting in graves, till we have suffered to the point at which we cry out that we have had enough. There will be a day when in presence of the useless thing we shall say, with something amounting to one accord, "It must stop." That day will be the beginning of the end of the age-long curse to which we still submit ourselves. In the language of St. Paul, "The last enemy to be destroyed is death," leaving us with the belief that, when we have progressed to the overthrow of other forces opposed to us, we shall go on to the overthrow of this one—and that it will be overthrown.

XVII

From one kind of fear this reasoning has almost entirely delivered me—that of being taken away in the midst of my responsibilities, and before my work is done. I am not so audacious as to say that it may not happen; but only that, reasoning as I do, I am no longer a prey to apprehensions on the point. They used to come to me, not like the money-fear, an abiding visitant, but in spells of intense dread.

I suppose that most men with families, and much unfinished business, know this dread, and have suffered from it. You think of the home you have built up, and of what it would be without you. You think of your wife, grappling with a kind of difficulty to which she is unaccustomed. You think of your children who turn to you as their central point, and who would be left without your guidance. You think of other duties you have undertaken, and wonder who will carry them through. You seem to be so essential to everyone and everything; and yet, you have been told, it may be the Will of God to remove you from them, and either let your plans collapse, or put their execution on the shoulders of someone else.

I am not so presumptuous as to say that for me this may not happen. I only say that I do not think it will. I do not think so because, according to my judgment, He having helped me to go as far as I have gone, will help me to finish my task before giving me another one.

My task, I think, He must estimate as I do. That is, my duties to others being not wholly of my choosing, but having come to me according to what I may call His weighing and measuring, I take them to be the duties He would have me perform. If so, He would naturally have me perform them till I come to the place where I can reasonably lay them down.

Therefore, I dismiss the fear of untimely separation from my appointed work. Such a separation may come; but if it does, it will probably come by some such means as I have briefly tried to sketch; my own mistakes; the mistakes of others; the effect of race-pressure. In any case, my personal resistance, it seems to me, is made the stouter by feeling that my tasks are His tasks, and so that so long as I am needful to their accomplishment, I remain. If I go, it will be because He has the succession of events so planned as to reduce collapse, failure, or suffering to a minimum.

XVIII

B. The thought that the minute after death will only be another little step in Growth, to be followed by another and then another, as we are used to growing here, greatly diminishes one's shrinking at the change.

It is entirely a modern thought. The past, even of a few centuries ago, never entertained it. It is doubtful if it was mentally prepared to entertain it, or evolve the idea.

This is not to depreciate our fathers' mental powers. Different generations have different gifts. One age works along one line, another along another. The past had a certain revelation of truth; but the revelation of truth did not end with the past. Our ancestors received as much as they could take. What, it seems, they were unable to take was anything which made death less horrible. We may say, in fact, that they didn't want it. They liked having death made horrible. Many people like it still. The mitigation of that horror they condemn, resent, and often ascribe to the devil.

And yet there is a tendency to see light through this gloom, and to seek views of death more in the line of common sense than those which have come down to us. It is not a strong tendency, but it exists. It exists in the face of opposition on the part of those religious conservatives who think conservatism and orthodoxy the same thing; and it runs the gauntlet of the sneers and jeers of the materially minded who make common cause with the old guard of the churches; but it exists. It exists, and goes forward, becoming a factor in the thought-life of our time.

It is not yet two hundred years since the plea was put forth on behalf of mankind that, in the administration of divine justice, no one suffers less than he deserves, but also that no one suffers more.

The hostility to this seemingly harmless teaching was of the most intense. There is hostility to it still, but mild as compared with that felt by our great-great-grandfathers. That no one should suffer less than he deserves went without saying; but that no one should suffer more was declared a black heresy. As there are those who declare it a black heresy to-day, it may be worth while, in the interests of the conquest of fear, to say a word as to the relation of God and punishment.

XIX

To my mind it is chiefly verbal.

It is permissible to say that there is no such thing as punishment; there are only wrong results. It depends upon your way of putting it. The wrong method produces wrong results in proportion as it is wrong. Wrong results mean wrong conditions; and wrong conditions mean suffering. You may call this the law of God, but it is the law of anything. It is not positive law, it is negative. As a matter of fact, God does not need to put forth a law on the point since everything works that way.

What we call sin is simply a wrong method. It may be a wrong method meant to produce wrong; or it may be a wrong method in the hope of producing right. In any case it brings its consequence in pain.

That consequence may be corrected in this phase of our being, or it may be carried over into the next. Carried over into the next the individual, according to our ancestral teaching, comes under the sentence in which our fathers delighted as "damnation." Not only did damnation involve the most fiendish torture the Almighty could invent, but the torture was inflicted, without an instant of relief, throughout the eons of eternity.

I recall a sermon to which I listened as a boy of nine. It was on a summer's evening, when the windows of the church were open. A moth fluttered about a light. The church stood at the foot of a mountain. The preacher was trying to explain to us the eternal duration of God's punishment. "Think of that moth," he said, "carrying away one grain of sand from that mountain, and going off for a million years, after which it would return and take away another grain. And think of it keeping this up, one grain every million years, till the whole mountain was removed. Well, that would be only a moment as compared with the time you would be in hell."

On the generations comforted and fortified by this sort of teaching I have no comment to make; but we of another generation should surely not be reproved for moving away from it. We move away from it in the direction of common sense, since common sense must be an attribute of the Universal Father as it is of the wiser among mankind.

XX

I revert, then, to my statement that God's relation to punishment is chiefly verbal. His "wrath against sin" is a way of "putting it." If you can best express the suffering which springs from wrong methods as "God's wrath" you are at liberty so to express yourself; but we should not lose sight of the fact that the wrong methods produce the suffering, and not an outburst of fury on the part of One who is put before us as Love.

The fact that the Hebrew writers often used a vivid form of warning and invective is not a reason why we should keep on doing it. The Hebrew writer was a primitive speaking to primitives. Meaning what we mean, he required a stronger, fiercer vocabulary than we ever need. In saying this I am not dodging the issue; I am stating a fact which rules in all historical interpretation. To make the phraseology of two thousand years before Christ the literal expression of the thought of two thousand years after Him is to be archaic beyond reason. Having grasped a principle, we phrase it in the language of our time.

The language of our time makes, on the whole, for restraint, sobriety, and exactitude of statement. Few of our habits modify themselves more constantly and more rapidly than our forms of speech. Not only does each generation find something special to itself, but each year and each season. To me it seems that much of our misunderstanding of God springs from the effort to fix on Him forevermore the peculiarities we infer from the idiom of five thousand years ago. Only to a degree does that idiom convey to us what is conveyed to those who heard it as a living tongue; and of that degree much is lost when it percolates through translation. To cling to words when all we need is to know principles, clothing them in our own way, seems to me not only absurd in fact but lamentable in result. I venture to think that more people have been alienated from God by a pious but misapplied verbal use than were ever estranged from Him by sin.

XXI

Our ancient Hebrew predecessors understood God in their own way. We understand Him in the same way, but with the clarification wrought by the intervening years of progress. In other words, they bequeath us a treasure which we are free to enrich with our own discoveries.

Among our own discoveries is a clearer comprehension of pain as resulting from wrong methods, and of God's detachment from pain. More and more, punishment becomes a concept we reject. Even in our penal institutions, which have been for so many centuries a barbarous token of our incompetence, we begin to substitute for punishment something more nearly akin to cure. If we find mere vengeance unworthy of ourselves we must find it unworthy of the Universal Father. If we concede to the criminal the right to a further chance we concede it to ourselves. If we recognise the fact that the sinner on earth may redeem himself, working from error towards righteousness, the same principle should rule in the whole range of existence. There is nothing about the earth-life to make it the only phase of effort and probation. Effort and probation are probably conditions of eternity. They will be in our next experience as they have been in this, leading us on from strength to strength.

XXII

One main difference between the mind of the past and the modern mind is that the mind of the past tended to be static, while the mind of to-day is more and more attuned to a dynamic universe. Civilisation before the nineteenth century was accustomed to long periods with relatively little change. Most people spent their entire lives in the same town or the same countryside. In the class in which they were born they lived and died, with little thought of getting out of it. This being so they looked for the same static conditions after death as they saw before it. A changeless heaven appalled them with no sense of monotony, nor did a changeless hell do anything to shake their nerves. Their nerves were not easily shaken. They were a phlegmatic race, placid, unimaginative, reposeful.

Because we of to-day are more restless it does not follow that our views should be truer. We only know they are truer because we are so much nearer the truth than they had the opportunity to come. We prove that we are nearer the truth by our greater command of the Father's resources. If our whole horizon of truth were not broadened, we could not possess this command.

XXIII

Changing our static conception of life to that of a dynamic will to unfold, we see the climax we commonly call death as only a new step in unfoldment. Whatever I have been, the step must be one in advance. It would not be in accord with creative energy that I should go backward. The advance may entail suffering, since it is probable that it will give me a heightened perception of the wrong in my methods; but there are conditions in which suffering signifies advance.

And yet if I suffer it can only be with what I may call a curative suffering. It will be suffering that comes from the recognition of mistake; not the hopeless anguish of the damned. Having learned "how not to do it," I perceive "how to do it"—and go on.

But the perception of "how to do it" is precisely what most of us have been acquiring. I venture to think that few of us will come face to face with death without being more or less prepared for it. Life is so organised that, at its worst, all but the rare exceptions make progress daily, through obedience to the laws of righteousness.

In saying this we must count as righteousness not merely the carrying out of a rule of thumb laid down by man's so-called morality, or the technical regulations prescribed by the churches for the use of their adherents; we must include every response to every high call. We must remember that all a man does in the way of effort to be a good son, a good brother, a good husband, a good father, a good workman, a good citizen, is of the nature of slowly creeping forward. Above every other form of training of the self this endeavour determines a man's spiritual standing, and his state of worthiness. He may know some failure in each of these details; and yet the fact that in the main he is set—as I am convinced the great majority are set—toward fulfilling his responsibilities helps him to be ready when the time comes to put the material away.

The great common sense of the nations brought us to this perception during the years when the young men of the world were going down like wheat before the reaping machine. For the most part, doubtless, they were young men in whom the ladies who attend our churches would have seen much to reprimand. The moral customs of their countries were possibly held by them lightly. The two points which constitute pretty nearly all of American morality they may have disregarded. And yet we felt that their answer to the summons, which to them at least was a summons to sacrifice, showed them as men who had largely worked out their redemption. Whatever our traditions, we were sure that those who were ready to do anything so great could go to the Father without fear.

But war calls for no more than a summing up and distillation of the qualities we cultivate in peace. These men were ready because homes, offices, banks, shops, factories, and farms had trained them to be ready. So they are training all of us. Traditions help; the churches help; but when it comes to the directing of the life toward righteousness—the effort to do everything rightly—no one thing has the monopoly.

XXIV

Going to the Father without fear! All the joy of life seems to me to hang on that little phrase. I used it just now of the young men who passed over from the battlefield; but I used it there with limitations. Going to the Father without fear is a privilege for every minute of the day. More and more knowledge of the Father is the progress for which we crave, since more knowledge of the Father means a fuller view of all that makes up the spiritual universe. Into that knowledge we are advancing every hour we live; into that knowledge we shall still be advancing at the hour when we die. The Father will still be showing us something new; the something new will still be showing us the Father.

It will be something new, as we can receive it. He who can receive little will be given little; he who can receive much will be given much. In growth all is adjusted to capacity; it is not meant to shock, force, or frighten. The next step in growth being always an easy step, I can feel sure of moving onwards easily—"from strength to strength," in the words of one of the Songs for the Sons of Korah, "until unto the God of gods appeareth everyone of them in Zion."[33]

The Fear Of Death And Abundance Of Life

I

After all, the conquest of fear is largely a question of vitality. Those who have most life are most fearless. The main question is as to the source from which an increase of life is to be obtained.

An important psychological truth was involved when our Lord made the declaration, "I am come that they might have life, and that they might have it more abundantly." This, I think, was the first plain statement ever made that life was a quantitative energy; that it is less or more dynamic according to the measure in which the individual seizes it. But once more the Caucasian has stultified the meaning of Jesus of Nazareth by evaporating it to the tenuous wisp which he understands as spiritual. Between the pale ghost of such spiritual life as he has evoked from the Saviour's words and manly and womanly vigour in full-blooded exercise he has seen no connection.

II

Few of us do see a connection between strength of spirit and strength of limb; but it is there. I am not saying that a strong spirit cannot coexist with a feeble frame; but the feeble frame is a mistake. It is the result of apprehension and misapprehension, and bred of race-fear. The strong spirit would have put forth a strong frame if we had given it a chance. Abundant life must be life, healthy, active, and radiant. It should show the life-principle no longer driven from sea to land, and from land to air, or battling with a million foes, but vigorous and triumphant.

This vigour and triumph we ought to work into our point of view, so kneading it into our subconsciousness. Strong in proportion as our subconsciousness is strong, fearless in proportion as our subconsciousness is fearless, the going from strength to strength becomes a matter of course to us. Urging us on in sheer joy of power, abundance of life becomes still more abundant through the indwelling of the life-principle. That mystic resistless force, which has fashioned already so many forms, is forever at work fashioning a higher type of man.

Each one of us is that higher type of man potentially. Though we can forge but little ahead of our time and generation, it is much to know that the Holy Ghost of Life is our animating breath, pushing us on to the overcoming of all obstacles. For me as an individual it is a support to feel that the principle which was never yet defeated is my principle, and that whatever the task of to-day or to-morrow I have the ability to perform it well. The hesitation that may seize me, or the questioning which for an instant may shake my faith, is but a reminder that the life-principle is not only with me, but more abundantly with me in proportion to my need. My need is its call. The spasm of fear which crosses my heart summons it to my aid. It not only never deserts me, but it never delays, and is never at a loss for some new ingenuity to meet new requirements. "From strength to strength" is its law, carrying me on with the impetus of its own mounting toward God.

III

And the impetus of its own mounting toward God is not confined to what we view as the great things of life. Between great and small it makes no distinction. It is as eager on behalf of the man behind a counter as on that of him who is governing a country. The woman who has on her shoulders the social duties of an embassy, or the financial cares of a great business, has it no more at her command than she who is nursing her baby or reckoning her pennies to make both ends meet. It rushes to the help of all. Wherever there is duty or responsibility it is begging at the doors of our hearts to be let in, to share the work and ease the burden.

As I get up each morning, it is there. As I plan my day while I dress myself, it is there. As I think with misgiving of some letter I tremble at receiving, or with distaste at some job I must tackle before night, it is there.

It is there, not only with its help, but with its absolute knowledge of the right way for me to act. The care that worries me may be so big as to involve millions of other people's money, or it may be as small as the typing of a letter; but the right way of fulfilling either task is pleading to be allowed to enter my intelligence. My task is its task. My success will be its success. My failure will react on it, since failure sets back by that degree the whole procession of the ages. Whether I am painting a great masterpiece or sewing on a button my success is essential to the Holy Ghost of Life.

IV

So I, the individual, try to confront each day with the knowledge that I am infused with a guiding, animating principle which will not let me drop behind, or lose my modest reward, so long as I trust to the force which carries me along. By trusting to it I mean resting on it quietly, without worrying, without being afraid that it will fail me. "Fret not thyself, else shalt thou be moved to do evil."[34] By doing evil, I presume is meant making a mistake, taking the wrong course. If, however great the cause, I fret myself I disturb the right conditions.

By disturbing the right conditions I choke off the flow of the life-principle through my energies.

V

At a moment when the little buffer state between Egypt and Assyria was afraid of being overrun by the one or the other it was frantically casting about to decide with which it would throw in its lot. "With neither," a great prophet thundered in the ears of the people. "In calmly resting your safety lieth; in quiet trust shall be your strength."[35]

My small experience in the conquest of fear can be condensed into these four words: Calmly resting! quiet trust! That amid the turmoil of the time and the feverishness of our days it is always easy I do not pretend. Still less do I pretend that I accomplish it. I have said, a few lines above, that I tried. Trying is as far as I have gone; but even trying is productive of wonderful results.

VI

Least of all do I claim to have covered the whole ground, or to have discussed to its fulness any one of the points which I have raised. Whole regions of thought which bear on my subject—such as psychology, philosophy, and religion as I understand the word—I have carefully endeavoured to avoid. My object has been to keep as closely as possible to the line of personal experience, which has a value only because it is personal. Telling no more than what one man has endeavoured to work out, what I have written seeks no converts. Though, for the sake of brevity, it may at times seem to take a hortatory tone, it is a record and no more. In it the reader will doubtless find much to correct, and possibly to reject; and this must be as it happens. What I hope he will neither correct nor reject is the sincerity of the longing to find God's relations to the phenomena of life, and the extent to which the phenomena of life reflect God.

VII

In the end we come back to that, the eternal struggle whereby that which is unlike God becomes more and more like Him. In watching the process, and taking part in it, there is, when all is said and done, a sense of glorious striving and success. With each generation some veil which hid the Creator from the creature is torn forever aside. God, who is always here, is seen a little more clearly by each generation as being; here. God, who ever since His sun first rose and His rain first fell has been making Himself known to us, is by each generation a little better understood. God, whom we have tried to lock up in churches or banish to Sundays and special holy days, is breaking through all our prohibitions, growing more and more a force in our homes and our schools, in our shops and our factories, in our offices and our banks, in our embassies, congresses, parliaments, and seats of government. Into His light we advance slowly, unwillingly, driven by our pain; but we advance.

The further we advance the more we perceive of power. The more we perceive of power the more we are freed from fear. The more we are freed from fear the more exultantly we feel our abundance of life. The more exultantly we feel our abundance of life the more we reject death in any of its forms. And the more we reject death in any of its forms the more we reflect that Holy Ghost of Life which urges us on from conquest to conquest, from strength to strength, to the fulfilling of ourselves.

Footnotes

[1] The Book of Isaiah.

[2] First Book of Samuel.

[3] Book of Daniel.

[4] The Book of Psalms.

[5] The Book of Psalms.

[6] Epistle to the Ephesians.

[7] Book of Psalms.

[8] Most of the quotations from the New Testament are taken from a recent translation, "The New Testament in Modern Speech," by R.F. Weymouth and E. Hampden-Cook.

[9] St. John

[10] The Book of Psalms.

[11] Epistle to the Romans.

[12] Acts of the Apostles.

[13] The Book of Deuteronomy.

[14] Various Old Testament Sources.

[15] The Book of Psalms.

[16] The Book of Psalms.

[17] Acts of the Apostles.

[18] St. Matthew.

[19] Epistle to the Romans.

[20] St. John.

[21] St. John.

[22] Epistle to the Ephesians.

[23] Second Epistle to the Corinthians.

[24] St Paul's Second Epistle to Timothy.

[25] St. Luke.

[26] St. Luke.

[27] The Book of Genesis.

[28] St. Luke.

[29] St. Luke.

[30] St. Luke.

[31] St Matthew.

[32] Epistle to the Romans.

[33] The Book of Psalms.

[34] The Book of Psalms.

[35] The Book of Isaiah.